Death by Despair

american
university
studies

Series VII
Theology and Religion

Vol. 245

PETER LANG
New York • Washington, D.C./Baltimore • Bern
Frankfurt am Main • Berlin • Brussels • Vienna • Oxford

Ramón Martínez de Pisón

Death by Despair

Shame and Suicide

PETER LANG
New York • Washington, D.C./Baltimore • Bern
Frankfurt am Main • Berlin • Brussels • Vienna • Oxford

Library of Congress Cataloging-in-Publication Data

Martínez de Pisón L., Ramón.
Death by despair: shame and suicide / Ramón Martínez de Pisón.
p. cm. — (American university studies.
Series VII, Theology and religion; v. 245)
Includes bibliographical references.
1. Shame—Religious aspects—Christianity. 2. Suicide—Religious aspects—
Christianity. 3. Death—Religious aspects—Christianity. I. Title. II. Series.
BT714.M34   152.4'4—dc22   2006000638
ISBN 0-8204-6382-5
ISSN 0740-0446

Bibliographic information published by **Die Deutsche Bibliothek**.
Die Deutsche Bibliothek lists this publication in the "Deutsche
Nationalbibliografie"; detailed bibliographic data is available
on the Internet at http://dnb.ddb.de/.

Author photo on back cover © Dennis Brunet

© 2006 Peter Lang Publishing, Inc., New York
29 Broadway, New York, NY 10006
www.peterlang.com

For all who have been wounded by shame and suicide,
that they might find inner peace

Contents

Foreword

J. Harold Ellens

The interface between psychology, religion, and spirituality has been of great interest to scholars for a century. In the last three decades a broad popular appetite has developed for books which make practical sense out of the sophisticated research on these three subjects. Ramón Martínez de Pisón has given us a volume on shame and suicide which identifies, analyzes, and describes the issues that deal with psychological factors at play in the way religion and spirituality function in persons with self-destructive types of personal suffering.

This book is for the general reader, the local library, and the undergraduate university student. I have spent an entire professional lifetime focused specifically upon research into the function of psychology in religion and spirituality. These matters are of the highest urgency in human affairs today when religious motivation seems to be playing an increasing role, constructively and destructively, in the arena of social ethics, national politics, and world affairs.

Death by Despair: Shame and Suicide addresses issues that are of universal concern but at the same time very personal and close to home. The author has seen that it is urgently necessary to discover what the psychopathological factors are that so shape and distort personal psychology and spirituality as to prompt terminal acts against oneself. This is an urgent and timely work, the motivation for which is needed by the entire world today, as we increasingly witness the unfolding of the all too common personal and family tragedy of suicide. What is going on in these cases? How are we to understand, stop, and heal this lethal wound in individuals and society? Martínez de Pisón has found some answers and shares them with us in a remarkably readable description through his own personal pilgrimage of anguish.

Much of the impact of the great religions upon human life and culture has been redemptive and of great good. It is urgent, therefore, that we discover and understand better what the psychological forces are which empower people of faith and genuine spirituality to give themselves to all the creative and constructive enterprises which, throughout the centuries, have made of human life the humane, ordered, prosperous, and beautiful experience it can be at its best. Surely the forces for good in both psychology and spirituality far exceed the powers and proclivities toward the destructive that we too often see in our world today.

Martínez de Pisón's work relates intimately to a line of experience which has woven itself throughout my life from very early in my development. I am particularly enthusiastic for this volume because I am confident that the same serendipitous connection with the content of this book will be true for everyone who picks it up and reads it. My childhood developed under the pall of death. When I was five I lost a brother and a sister, children who died pathetically of childhood illness which could not be remedied in those days of the Great Depression. That same year my dearest friend of all, the five year old girl from across the country road, burned to death as I stood helplessly watching. We had spoken joyfully of starting school together that September, but on August 3, 1937 she caught her frilly little dress on fire in the kitchen and suddenly she was gone forever. It was an accident, not a suicide, but it seared my soul with a permanent wound, the throbbing pain of which is awakened with every child that dies and every hopeless, helpless soul that contemplates self-destruction.

Two years later I determined upon my life's vocation. I committed myself, quite consciously, to a life of care for the pain and suffering I seemed to perceive everywhere around me in those years. It actually took me a quarter century before I could express my feelings and coherently formulate my understanding of these early shaping events. By then I was already established on the trajectory of my life's calling and in my work of the helping professions. I studied theology, psychology, and pastoral care. I took a commission in the US Army Chaplaincy where I thought the pain and need was most accute, and I was deployed overseas when the master story with all its meaning and recovered memories finally came into focus for me.

It turned out that in this process a key event directly related to the subject of Martínez de Pisón's book proved to be a turning point. After graduating from high school in 1949 I reported for my pre-seminary program at Calvin College that fall. One of my first encounters at college was with Professor Henry Van Til, academic counselor for pre-seminary students. I knew little about a college curriculum but expressed interest in taking a course in philosophy with the noted Professor Harry Jellema. Unbeknown to me in my freshman *naïveté*, Van Til had a rather basic and vigorous philosophical antipathy for Jellema's liberal perspective. Thus he tended to steer students away from Jellema's courses.

Van Til strongly recommended that I consider instead a course in Abnormal Psychology, offered by the very entertaining Professor John Daling. Van Til, himself a former pastor, and now a professor of theology, followed up his urgent suggestion with a persuasive illustration. He told me in great detail of a life-shaping experience he had in his first parish when one of his parishioners had taken her life. He described how un-prepared he had been for ministry to the grieving family, the despair he felt about having missed the clues of her suffering and self-destructiveness, and the quandary into which the entire experience had thrown him regarding the inadequacy of his own theology and personal spirituality. He drew his story to an eloquent climax with the sobering declaration that he had never gotten over what he always remembered as his failure.

There was a sturdy providence in the way in which that event harnessed and drove the forces of my vocation that had been set at age seven. That early training, that I followed in pursuit of the mutual illumination that theology and psychology offer each other, has been the work of my life every since.

The trajectory of my life has been a straight line from the tragedies of my fifth year, through my vocational decision at age seven, and my development and work to this moment and this message in this Foreword. At every turn of the road in those 68 years I have been called upon to bring help and consolation to hopeless persons set upon self-destruction. Martínez de Pisón's book has a very familiar beat and tune for me. It is a word of consolation set to the chords of a funeral dirge.

As a child I found completely mystifying my father's stories about the suicides of notable people who had lost their wealth in the stock market crash three years before my birth, and again in the bank holiday the year after my birth. After fifty years of pastoral ministry and clinical work, I understand the reasons for their suicides. Great tragedy can cause utter loneliness, isolation, helplessness, and despair. Martínez de Pisón examines these factors with great understanding. In every phase of my life's work the mystifying presence of persons attempting suicide has raised its painful head. Recently, an acquaintance of mine, a General Officer in the US Army, having invested his daughter's life savings for her and lost it in the stock market down turn, found the helplessness and despair of it too impossible to endure and hung himself. A gentle woman I knew well, having lived for thirty years with a cantankerous husband whose sour soul had poisoned their sons' psyches, could not go on, and overdosed.

The list could be extended to unfortunate length. We all know the stories from personal experience. Everyone's life has been touched by this horror. All of us go through it feeling rage and guilt for our own inability to have noticed sooner and done more. During the destructive social revolution from 1965 to 1974 I buried 37 overdose victims and 34 motor cycle victims, all young people, all drug related, all suicides, I am sure. Suicide is everywhere, and the statistics describe only the tip of the iceberg. It is likely that more self-inflicted deaths go unreported than reported. A conspiracy of cultural silence insures that every other explanation for death is given whenever possible; rather than acknowledging forthrightly the incredible frequency of self-destructive acts. Martínez de Pisón's book is about the omnipresence of suicidal behavior, overt attempts, and their tragic consequences. He analyses the issues carefully and makes a profound plea for societal awareness, honesty, and concern which will help us to see the human pain around us and intervene on time with life-saving passion and compassion.

Certainly the reason why we have not done a better job in our society of the care of those who are on self-destructive paths lies in the fact that we have not made it our responsibility as a culture to understand better the dynamics of suicide. This is the great virtue of this present book and its author. He has taken up the challenge to be responsible regarding this grievous and deadly matter and to help *us* all be more responsible, as well. One of the points Martínez de Pisón addresses is the role of religious perspectives and faith traditions in suicide. His treatment of this matter is illuminating and detailed. His understanding of the role of shame in religion and in suicide is incredibly important and genuinely helpful.

What might be added to his insights in this regard is the contention which has often seemed to me central to the relationship of religion and suicide. Personal spirituality is both the source and the expression of religion. Spirituality is best defined as the irrepressible inner human hunger or quest for meaning in life. This definition applies regardless of the faith tradition in which one's spirituality is being worked out. In this sense every human being is intensely spiritual, though some cultivate its fulfillment more consciously and overtly than others.

Spirituality is part of the essence of being human. I suspect that it may be the case that the self-destructive ideation or action of suicide may be not only the result of an utter loss of meaning; but it may well be the choice of an alternative quest for meaning. It may be a course chosen when the meaning of the standard sources has come to seem hopeless or unfulfilling. This sense of meaninglessness may derive from the mental illness of psychoses in which the person's perception of reality is twisted away from the way things really are. It may come from being overwhelmed by tragedy. Or it may derive from a complete inner emptiness resulting from a life wasted on the distractions that prevent learning, that undermine achievement, that distort or obstruct mental development, that render one insensitive to a sense of the beauty of things, that cause a vacuous sense of self, and that leave one lost from any sense of history.

It was clear to me while attending the pastoral and psychological concerns of the families afflicted by the tragic suicides of the social revolution of the late 1960s that the main problem for those self-destructive young people was the last of those three reasons for meaninglessness. It was a time when students did not learn, families did not share, children learned no respect or discipline, thus self-discipline became a lost art and the inevitable self-destruction took its place in the lives of all too many vacuous and empty youth. It was as though Camus and Sartre had written the score for their tragic opera; and as a result the only tune they knew was *No Exit!* Unfortunately that cultural tune continues to play in our world. The consequences continue to be dead end streets for to many our youth.

What has often worried me, however, in the backdrop to all this, is a more sinister possibility in the relationship between spirituality, religion, and suicide. Western Religions might be referred to as the action religions of the world that express themselves externally in social institutions and actions. These may be distinguished from Eastern Religions, which tend to be passive and emphasize interiority. The three main Western Religions, Judaism, Christianity, and Islam, all derive directly from the literature and ideas of ancient Israelite religion, expressed in the Hebrew Bible, or Old Testament. From this source has been carried over into the Judaism, Christianity, and Islam of the last millennium and a half a specific set of ideas which have proven violent and destructive. Surely this fact is not unrelated to the prominence and irrationality of suicide in the West.

The ancient idea which pervades the three religions and grounds them in violence is the notion that what we are up against in life is a cosmic conflict in which the forces of transcendental good and evil are ranged against each other in an eternal and mortal conflict that plays out on the battleground of history and the human heart. God and the anti-god, good and evil, God and devil, are the transcendental protagonist and antagonist. They fight with approximately equal force and power, and it remains to be seen which will triumph. In this contest both God and Satan resort readily to utter violence to solve ultimate problems with final solutions. Regardless of whether the problem and solution are the 1) extermination of the ancient Canaanites or 2) of contemporary Palestinians, or 3) God being so angry that he must kill us all or kill his "beloved son" or 4) kill the enemies of his beloved son, or 5) God being so intent on the purity of the Umma of Islam that he must wreak a Jihad against every Infidel or fly planes into the World Trade Center, the matter is all the same. It all derives from the cosmic conflict idealized in ancient Israelite religion.

This tragic notion of history and religion is unimaginably unfortunate on two counts. First, it is a lie. There is no data on which to ground a worldview with this cosmic conflict at the core. There is no cosmic force of evil. The only evil that exists is what we do to each other. That is plain and simple. The only thing "out there" is the God of universal grace and mercy. Second, if God is portrayed as tending to solve ultimate problems with the final solutions of ultimate violence, what hope or help is there for the helpless and hopeless person toying around the edges of self-destruction. If he or she mimics God, is not the violence of suicide all the more likely? How much does the sick side of religion feed the tragedy of violent dead-ends.[1] The Pulitzer Prize winning author, Jack Miles, wrote a book on the New Testament, entitled *Christ: A Crisis in the Life of God.*[2] The title of the German edition tellingly refers to the suicide of God.

What awful primordial archetypes in the deep and primitive caverns of the unconscious human psyche are given life or content or reinforcement by the violent metaphors of religion? How do they torture and distort the visions and ideations of the human spirit's moments of extremity? Can we turn those around and replace them with the metaphors of grace? Are there psychological and spiritual sources and resources in us for healing, hope, and life instead of death and self-destruction? Those are the questions Ramón Martínez de Pisón undertakes to answer in this thoughtful, useful book.

Notes

[1]   Ellens (Ed.), 2004.

[2]   Miles, 2001. In 1997 Miles published *God: A Biography*, which was on the Hebrew Bible and won the Pulitzer Prize.

Acknowledgments

I would like to thank all those whose contributions made this book possible. André Paris, Chief Librarian at Saint Paul University, found important research on shame and suicide. Daniel Hurtubise, Library Technician, was resourceful in acquiring documents from other Libraries.

I owe a debt of gratitude to my colleagues at Saint Paul University who corrected the manuscript and gave me useful advice: Normand Bonneau, J. Kevin Coyle, Terry Gall, Miriam K. Martin, James Pambrun, and Dale M. Schlitt.

I am also grateful to Anne Éthier, Colin Levangie, and Anne Louise Mahoney for their help in refining the chapters, and for making insightful remarks upon their content.

To my friends Richard G. Cote, Carl Kelly, and J. Lorne MacDonald, who had to endure the many times I spoke about shame and suicide, I thank them for their support and encouragement. Their comments on the evolving manuscript were indispensable.

I wish to thank Dr. J. Harold Ellens, for writing the Foreword. Furthermore, he has been a source of inspiration to me, both in his valuable suggestions for improving the text and in his encouragement to incorporate my own experience of becoming empowered by my healing process.

I would like to thank Georgia Prince, Manager, Rights and Permissions, Kluwer Academic/Plenum Publishers, who granted me permission to reproduce my article "Shame, Death, and Dying," published in 2002 in *Pastoral Psychology, 51, 1,* 27–40, sections of which appear in the first and the last two chapters of this book.

Finally, I wish to express my appreciation to Anne Chevalier and Audrey Wells from Novalis for helping prepare the manuscript for publication.

This book has been published with the financial support of the Publication Grants Program of Saint Paul University (Ottawa, Canada).

Introduction

Suicide is one of the leading causes of violent death in societies throughout the world.[1] In addition to the deceased, each suicide affects several people: relatives, friends, neighbors, and colleagues. It also affects all their enterprises.

Statistics on suicide raise serious concerns, even though they cannot fully reflect the complete reality of this tragedy. There are a number of reasons for the limited value of the figures. First, there are considerable differences between countries on what defines a death as suicide. This raises questions concerning the "reliability and validity of death certification."[2] Secondly, many deaths by suicide are disguised as accidental deaths. Thirdly, besides the fact that many insurance companies do not cover death by suicide, there are two points which must be noted. There exist social, cultural and religious stigma attached to suicide. Moreover, many suicides among old people are under-reported for understandable reasons: avoidance of "embarrassment, shame and/or guilt for the family; the reluctance of nursing homes to report suicides because of negative publicity; and the comparative lack of curiosity about deaths of older individuals."[3] Finally, there is a tendency to limit reports of suicides in order to prevent what some theories call "suicidality syndrome," namely, that the suicide of someone could lead others to imitate this deadly act "independently of the presence of psychiatric disorders."[4]

Despite the lack of accurate statistics, there is ample evidence that the mean age of those who commit or attempt suicide is steadily dropping. Adolescents in particular are at greatest risk.[5] By the time they reach their teens, young people often have already been confronted with very painful experiences, leading some of them to commit or to attempt suicide. Many lack the necessary skills to deal with stressful events in a healthy life-enhancing way.

At the other end of the lifespan the rate of suicide is also quite high. The last stage of human development is not necessarily one in which women and men always feel fulfilled. Despair, feelings of failure and uselessness, poverty, chronic health problems, social isolation or loneliness, and psychological vulnerabilities such as hopelessness, depression, alcoholism and other forms of substance abuse are frequent contributing factors to suicide among the elderly.[6]

A Theory of Coping

Common to all the above contributing factors is stress. Suicide and suicide-related events, such as the bereavement process of survivors, the attitudes of family members, friends, society, and positions of religious denominations on suicide, are among the most stressful experiences of life. Accordingly, learning to cope with these events in a positive way is essential. Richard S. Lazarus and Susan Folkman, in their book *Stress, Appraisal and Coping*, have developed an important theory dealing with the problem of coping with stress. They see coping as a process with different stages, displaying multiple functions. It involves personal and environmental "inhibitors of the effective use of coping resources."[7]

In the present study I expand Lazarus and Folkman's theory of coping with stress in order to show that toxic shame is one of the most important personal and environmental constraints inhibiting one's ability to cope, in a healthy way, with suicide and suicide-related events. In this sense, I use *constraints* in its negative connotation, even if, as Lazarus and Folkman recognize, "constraints can also be facilitative"[8] of the coping process. Many suicides result from a lack of coping skills for dealing with chronic shame in constructively. Excessive shame plays a negative role in human development. When experiencing unhealthy shame, one feels worthless, exposed to the invasive scrutiny and negative evaluation of others. It is therefore important not only to identify the sources of shame, but also to recognize how shame generates further shame through the process of internalization. The internalization of negative beliefs triggers a spiral of shame reactions that can lead to suicidal behavior.

For several years, I have been studying the importance of shame in human development, particularly in its connection with suicide. My first intuition centered around the relationship between shame, death, and dying.[9] Gradually, this first intuition developed into awareness of the relationship between shame and suicide. I then focused on the analysis of the current literature on shame and suicide, mainly from 1990 to 2000.

As a result I realize how little research has concentrated on the link between suicide and shame. The research that exists is expressed in such highly technical language that it is inaccessible to non-specialists. One is confronted with empirical/quantitative studies that do not reveal the human suffering involved in these events. Many times, people's deep feelings and experiences are lost in the quantifiable data. John R. Jordan points out that

> Simple quantitative measures of grief may not detect some of the thematic or qualitative differences . . . such as the heightened feelings of guilt and preoccupation with the

question of why the death occurred. These are more likely to be observed in qualitatively based research methodology that allows research participants to explain their experience to the researcher in their own words.[10]

It seems to me important to take into consideration the qualitative dimension of the research in order to direct attention to the relationships between shame and suicide that are not always evident in a quantitative presentation of information. It was also essential to make the results of my research available in an easily understandable form so as to foster a sensitivity to the human feelings of shame and self destruction.

A Preview of the Book

Therefore, in the first chapter, I present the role that chronic shame plays in suicide. Here, as throughout this book, the terms *chronic or dysfunctional shame, unhealthy shame, undue shame, excessive shame, toxic shame, negative shame,* and *pathological shame* mean about the same thing.

Another clarification is necessary. Donald L. Nathanson, in his book *Shame and Pride: Affect, Sex, and the Birth of the Self,* distinguishes between *affect, feeling,* and *emotion.* For him, *affect* means "the strictly biological portion of emotion."[11] *Feeling* "implies the presence of higher order mechanisms or components that allow knowledge and understanding. . . . [It suggests] that a person has some level of awareness that an affect has been triggered."[12] Finally, *emotion* refers to the combination of affect with memory: for example, when a present experience, such as embarrassment, "resembles one in which I was embarrassed last month, or last year, or frequently in a way I cannot alter, or in a relationship that resembles the one in which I find myself today."[13] However, in my own research on shame and suicide, I have found that many authors do not make a distinction between *affect, feeling,* and *emotion.*[14] For this reason, even taking into consideration the nuances adopted by Nathanson, I shall frequently use *feeling* and *emotion* synonymously.

The second chapter describes current approaches to shame as a factor in suicide. In these approaches, shame is inferred, or bypassed, and translated into other characteristics of the person, for example, alienation, hopelessness, depression, alcoholism, perfectionism and narcissism.

Following upon the initial presentation of the various negative consequences that excessive shame plays in suicide, the third chapter addresses the effectiveness of Lazarus and Folkman's theory of coping with stress, in its application to shame as a personal and environmental constraint, impeding the ability to deal with suicide in a healthy way. In this sense, religion will be considered as both *facilitative* of the process for coping with suicide in a positive way, and also as an *inhibitor* militating against using positive resources for dealing with suicide.

In an application of the theory of Lazarus and Folkman, the fourth chapter deals with the role that chronic or dysfunctional shame plays among those who attempted suicide and survived; the family and friends of those who committed suicide and who must pass through the bereavement process; and the stigma that society, culture, and different religious denominations continue to attach to suicide. Here, and throughout this study, *bereavement* refers to the entire process of coping with death; *mourning* signifies its social expression; and *grief* means the personal, feeling aspect of coping with death.[15]

In the fifth chapter I examine the importance of overcoming the negative influence that shame exercises in suicide and suicide-related events. Within this framework I shall stress the necessity of being reconciled with oneself, as well as the need to share with others one's innermost feelings and emotions in the context of changing social, cultural, and religious attitudes towards suicide.

Finally, in the last chapter I present my own experience of becoming empowered by healing. Thus, this book is also the fruit of my own personal and family experiences in dealing with the negative consequences of shame and suicide. Owning these experiences in my life is a way of giving them a voice. They allow a better understanding of what they were trying to tell me, or what I can learn from my own pain. I think that, as a professional, to share my own experience of healing may support others in dealing with their own suffering.

Like all research, this one has its limits. I do not claim to consider all the dimensions involved in suicide, nor will I introduce every possible connection between shame and suicide. Following Lazarus and Folkman, my purpose here is to present shame as a personal and environmental constraint against coping with suicide in a healthy way, a constraint that needs to be confronted and overcome.

A Vision for Healing Humans

In addition, although I dare to hope that this study may help sensitize the general population to the increasing reality of suicide, I am writing this book primarily in order that it may serve as a useful tool for those who must deal with this experience, such as survivors, psychiatrists, family doctors, nurses, psychologists, clergy, social workers and other professionals.

As a university professor and a Roman Catholic Priest, I have had to deal frequently with the pain and suffering of survivors over the loss of their loved ones, as well as with the resulting shame and stigma attached to suicide. These experiences impair the process of grieving and could even bring some survivors themselves to attempt suicide. My own personal and family experience and my pastoral work with survivors, therefore, has prompted me to write this book to provide a better understanding, a gradual lessening and eventual elimination of the influences of shame on suicide.

Notes

[1]   Conner, Duberstein, Conwell, Seidlitz, & Caine, 2001; DiFillippo & Overholser, 2000; Gunnell, 2000; Holden & Kroner, 2003; Leenaars & Connolly, 2001; McClelland, Reicher, & Booth, 2000; Westefeld et al., 2000.

[2]   Schmidtke et al., 1999, p. 87.

[3]   Klingler, 1999, p. 116.

[4]   Leonard, 2001, p. 465.

[5]   Ayyash-Abdo, 2002; Barber, 2001; Barrios, Everett, Simon, & Brener, 2000; Beautrais, 2000; DiFillippo & Overholser, 2000; Thomas, 2003.

[6]   Conwell, Dubertstein, & Caine, 2002; Corens & Hewitt, 1999; Hoxey & Shah, 2000; Klinger, 1999; Pritchard & Baldwin, 2002.

[7]   Lazarus & Folkman, 1984, p. 167.

[8]   Lazarus & Folkman, 1984, p. 167.

[9]   Martínez de Pisón, 2002.

[10]   Jordan, 2001, p. 96.

[11]   Nathanson, 1992, p. 40.

[12]   Nathanson, 1992, p. 50.

[13]   Nathanson, 1992, p. 50.

[14]   Feshbach, Weiner, & Bohart, 1996.

[15]   Parkes, 1985; Valente & Saunders, 1993.

Chapter I

Life and Death in Shame

The relationship between shame and suicide is not self-evident. One reason for this is that shame expresses itself in many different ways. Shame can have a positive role, as a defense mechanism, or as a way of recognizing our human vulnerability. Shame can also play a negative role as, for example, when it has a destructive influence on the development of self-esteem.

Shame does not necessarily manifest itself directly. Frequently it is evident indirectly in the way a person expresses himself or herself. This is what is called *unowned* or *bypassed shame*. The individual does not realize how shame influences his or her behavior.

Suicide often occurs when chronic shame overtakes a person. In these circumstances, suicide becomes a dysfunctional way of coping with undue shame, even if one admits that in some cultures, as in the Japanese culture, suicide is quite an acceptable and honorable way of dealing with shame.

The Many Faces of Shame

Shame, the so-called *invisible dragon*,[1] is among the least studied of the dimensions which affect human development. Dealing with it has become a taboo in Western society. As Gershen Kaufman emphasizes, "The cultural taboo surrounding human sexuality in an earlier age is thus matched by an equally pronounced taboo surrounding shame today."[2] This taboo, and the uneasiness that shame causes, are due to numerous factors.

Merle A. Fossum and Marylin J. Mason propose the image of the dragon to suggest the many faces of shame. These authors state that "the dragon possesses the power of metamorphosis and the gift of rendering itself invisible."[3] Shame's invisibility refers also to the difficulty of recognizing its presence in life and in human interactions because, as Patricia S. and Ronald T. Potter-Efron say, "shame is the most hidden of emotions,"[4] a state of affairs due in great part to the lack of an appropriate language for expressing the innermost emotions. According to Kaufman,

The failure to attend to shame until quite recently is partially the result of the failure of scientific languages that describe inner experience. Without an accurate language of the self, shame slips quickly into the background of awareness. Our competing psychological languages or theories also have oriented us more toward examining guilt. The consequent reification of guilt as a construct has unfortunately obscured the role of shame, hindering accurate perception of its impact and dynamic complexity. Finally, psychological theorists as well as practitioners have found it both easier and safer to explore "guilty" impulses rather than a "shameful" self.[5]

Shame and Guilt

The first thing that one must consider is the difference between shame and guilt. Shame is not guilt. Shame reaches to the core of the person in a way that actions do not.[6] Guilt does not affect the person as a whole, but is limited to one's actions,[7] as it is generated by "the fear of punishment and abandonment for the violation of moral values."[8] Hellen B. Lewis describes the role of the self in shame and guilt in the following terms:

> *Shame is about the self; guilt is about things.* Shame thus appears to be a "narcissistic" reaction evoked by a lapse from the ego ideal. An ego ideal is difficult to spell out rationally; shame thus can be a subjective, "irrational" reaction. Shame is about the whole self and is therefore "global". Guilt is more specific, being about events or things. Adults regard shame as an "irrational" reaction that is more appropriate to childhood, especially if it occurs outside the context of moral transgression.[9]

This matter was succinctly defined by Ellens in 1982. Guilt is a perceived state of failing before the law. Shame is the state of perceived failure before the face of some valued person or group. It is important, therefore, to avoid identifying *shame* with *guilt*, as has often happened, even though there are some connections between them.

Shame is conditioned by genetico-biological predispositions, and socio-historical, cultural, religious, gender, and age factors. For example, empirical research shows that women experience shame more frequently than men, while men usually experience guilt more often. Helen B. Lewis explains this difference, saying:

> In brief, I have suggested [in previous publications] that women's greater sociability and lesser aggression, taken together with their second-class status in the world of power, increase their tendency to the experience of shame. Men, in contrast, because of their lesser sociability and greater aggression, and their unfair position of superiority in the world of power, are more susceptible to guilt.[10]

Others, like Stephen Pattison, accentuate how it is possible that women, more than men, may have some genetic predispositions to shame, even if

Very little is known about genetic and biological predispositions to particular emotional responses or personality traits. However, if it is accepted that biological and other factors work together to shape personality, then a notional, if unclear, significance must be attached to this factor in the evolution of shame as an affective response and personality trait.[11]

Pattison recognizes that other factors such as, for example, socialization, may have more influence on the tendency of women toward shame than the genetico-biological. The process of women's socialization is deeply conditioned by cultural factors which often valorize submissiveness and obedience, self-blame, passivity, helplessness, and so forth in women, features that contribute to fostering shame-prone personalities.

These conditioning contexts manifest a plurality of standards, roles, goals and values by which people measure themselves as a whole. Consequently, "the totality of our emotional life, including the experience of shame, takes place in a social nexus."[12] This also means that the core of shame, together with guilt and pride, "involve[s] self-consciousness. It is not possible to feel shame without comparing one's action against one's standards or beliefs."[13] For Michael Lewis, "shame is not produced by any specific situation but rather by the individual's interpretation of a situation."[14] He goes on to say that the origins of shame are to be found in "the emergence of objective self-awareness."[15] Thus, according to Warren Breed,

> shame penetrates the whole self, occurring when the person is failing to accomplish a goal presented by the ego-ideal. . . . It is a real "shortcoming," exposing the self to the self and to the pitying gaze of others. . . . It is this exposure of the weakness of the self and its role performance in the eyes of significant others that hurts. Such a failure and the anticipation of negative reactions from other people constitute not only a source of anxiety but a disastrous blow to the self-esteem.[16]

Healthy Shame, Sick Shame

There is a positive, healthy view of shame. In this sense, shame plays an essential role in human development. It constitutes a protection of the self, of one's personal identity, in adverse circumstances, and it sets boundaries or limits that human beings should not trespass.[17] In this sense, too, one can consider the role that shame plays in religion. As Helen B. Lewis says, "In our Judeo-Christian heritage, shame, in the sense of humility, was (is) a principal emotion governing a person's loving relationship to God, as the story of Job attests. Job refused to blame God or himself for God's 'rejection' of him, preferring to remain humble and still loving."[18] This coincides with John Bradshaw's position regarding healthy shame: "Healthy shame," he says, "is the psychological foundation of humility. It is the source of spirituality."[19] Therefore, this first dimension of shame is called *modesty,*[20] *humility,*[21] and *respect* or *discretion shame,* that is, "It acts as an internalised defender of treasured social attitudes, values and behaviours."[22]

Furthermore, the consciousness of one's own fragility and vulnerability as a human being, together with the process of learning and maturing, are dimensions that generate a healthy sense of shame.[23] Shame is thus an authentic manifestation of being human. Pattison calls this second dimension *ontological shame:* "This may be characterised as shame that relates to being human and finding oneself to be limited and mortal. The state of being human, finite, mortal, embodied, dependent on others and so on involves fundamental shame."[24]

More commonly, however, shame is considered as having a degrading, dysfunctional, and pathological influence in a person's life. The adverse consequences of what can be called excessive shame appear in some of the well-known attitudes of the shame-prone person: "The desire to hide or to disappear. . . . Embarrassment and shyness. . . . The feeling that one is no good, inadequate, unworthy. It is a global statement by the self in relation to the self. And . . . we become the object as well as the subject of shame."[25]

Although generally fostered in infancy and childhood, "shame may and does occur in every stage of human development. Moreover, there appears to be no distinct, common source for the acquisition of shame."[26] Thus, according to Pattison,

> Any experiences that induce a sense of persistent inferiority, worthlessness, abandonment, weakness, abjection, unwantedness, violation, defilement, stigmatisation, unlovability and social exclusion are likely to be generative of chronic shame. Perhaps the lowest common denominator in all the factors outlined here is the experience of human individuals being dishonoured, disrespected or objectified. It is this kind of experience, from infancy onwards, that engenders people whose personalities, characters and attitudes are fundamentally shaped by chronic shame.[27]

Consequently, one must not speak about shame as having only *one* source; rather, one must recognize the *variety* of sources that favor its emergence.

For some authors, shame is "an inborn script"[28] or "one of the quintessential human emotions."[29] Its emergence is seen as linked "to unconscious fantasies."[30] According to Rizzuto, "*shame is related to a self evaluation* (ego and superego) *of being undeserving of a desired affective response.* It concerns the narcissistic component of any experience or fantasy, be it pre-oedipal, oedipal or post-oedipal. Behind the negative self-evaluation lurk the fears of the loss of the object and of loss of love."[31] For others, the most important element in the development of pathological shame is chemical addiction, and other dependencies, such as eating disorder, and the like.[32] At the very least, "these [addictions] are syndromes in which shame plays a central role."[33] If we are more aware of shame today, it is precisely because of increasing concerns about addictions in Western society[34] and improved understanding of the human emotional system.[35]

From a phenomenological point of view, shame is considered "within the context of human relationships rather than just 'within' the body."[36] Being rejected, humiliated or abandoned by significant others, and the "absence of approving reciprocity,"[37] is at the heart of chronic shame.[38] Hence, "for shame to occur there must be an emotional relationship between the person and the other such that the person cares about a negative evaluation by the other. In this affective tie the self does not feel autonomous or independent, but dependent and vulnerable to rejection."[39] These situations, particularly when they occur in infancy and early childhood, produce a child who is forever dissatisfied, experiences a lack of intimacy and, as a result, generates "compulsive/addictive behavior."[40]

For others, socio-historical and cultural contexts play an essential role in the origin of shame. According to Pattison,

> Shame may well be the most socially significant of all the phenomena that are commonly conceived as emotions. It is a socio-cultural phenomenon that reflects and refracts wider social trends and relationships. It helps to define social boundaries, norms and behaviours and signals the state of social bonds (Scheff 1997), as well as providing a powerful tool of social conformity and control. Thus shame is an indispensable and necessary part of the socio-emotional architecture of any social order. This does not prevent it from being a painful, difficult and alienating experience for some individuals and groups in society. Nor does it prevent the exploitation of shame for purposes of power and control by other individuals and groups.[41]

In the North American context, shame has been approached more from the standpoint of its influence on people's lives, as a personal dimension, and in relationships, rather than as an instrument of social control.

Many times, the person feels the shame of others as an in-dwelling within herself or himself because of particular events which are considered shameful, such as incest, crime, suicide, a particular illness, or a social and cultural incident. For this reason, the shame remains hidden, secret, or even denied.[42] These experiences, then, are deeply conditioned by society and culture.

Finally, a person must protect herself or himself against the feelings and emotions generated by shame. A person does this by developing a shield, namely, the tendency to be hidden from others. In the end, however, the person hides from his or her self by molding "a false identity out of this basic core. We become master impersonators. We avoid our core agony and pain and over a period of years, we avoid our avoidance."[43]

Integrating Shame into Life

Therefore, as the fifth chapter of this study will outline, one of the most important dimensions in dealing with shame in therapy is success or failure in bringing the client to recognize and to integrate his or her innermost feelings of shame into constructive life. Thus, "It is not possible to address shame in individuals if its presence is unrecognised."[44] Moreover, people must not only get in touch with their innermost feelings and emotions in order to overcome toxic shame, they must also be able to share them with significant others, recreating with them a positive network of relationships, because as Goldberg says, "the healing of shame requires the opportunity for genuine friendship. . . . [Accordingly,] people who lack or lose trusted friendship are vulnerable to the devastating effects of shame."[45]

Consequently, as James M. Harper and Margaret H. Hoopes indicate, "Trying to resolve issues of shame on one's own is usually counterproductive, since these issues are best resolved in the context of relationships that can be positively affirming and deal with issues of intimacy, dependency, and accountability."[46] In this sense, even to *confess* the events generating such destructive feelings, and to *forgive* oneself and another, can bring about a liberation from dysfunctional shame.[47] Thus, according to some theories, if at the origin of shame there is an undisclosed event which the person seeks to hide, then in order to be liberated from unhealthy shame the person must identify and externalize the destructive event which, like an internal poison, binds that person.[48]

Finally, as Pattison indicates, one needs "to address the social and political factors that create and exploit an unhelpful sense of shame and alienation on the level of institutions and communities."[49] This involves unmasking the negative consequences that shame plays as a way of social control. As we will now see, oftentimes one has to deduce the presence and the adverse influence of shame by its effects in people's lives and behaviors.

Bypassed Shame

Four principal authors will serve as guides for the following understanding of the importance of unowned or bypassed shame: Helen B. Lewis, Gershen Kaufman, Carl Goldberg, and Michael Lewis.

Helen B. Lewis was the first to speak about unacknowledged and bypassed shame. She says in this regard:

> I have also identified two somewhat different states of shame. One I call overt, unidentified or unacknowledged shame in which the person is in an acute state of self-hatred but without recognizing shame. The other state I call bypassed shame. In this case, the person is clearly dealing with shaming events and may even say that he or she is embarrassed but

without being caught up in shame feeling, except for a momentary jolt to the self. The person seems to be registering shame experience by incessant ideation about the role of the self in the shaming events–potency failure, for example, or some other shaming event, such as an anxiety state. The ideation of bypassed shame often passes easily into obsessive but insoluble guilty dilemmas.[50]

Thus, in the first situation, people are experiencing deeply the emotions that accompany shame, even if in an unidentified way. But in the second case, the person tries to cope with shame by passing it through the process of ideation and rationalization, without feeling the strong emotions characteristic of the presence of shame. Furthermore, it is easier for people to handle obsessive guilt dilemmas than to deal with the emotions of shame.

Gershen Kaufman, for his part, refers to another way in which we can recognize bypassed shame, namely, by noting addictive disorders. As indicated in the first part of this chapter, according to Kaufman addictions are syndromes intimately linked to shame. Therefore,

Addictive disorders comprise a third class of syndromes in which shame, either singly or in combination with other negative affects, plays a central role. The addiction functions as an escape from or sedation of these intolerable negative affects. Feelings of shame, for example, can be reduced through becoming addicted to something. Addiction sedates intense negative affect, but the addiction also reproduces shame, thereby reactivating the cycle. The addictive process repetitively reenacts a scene that recreates and intensifies shame. The objects are longed for repetitively, causing repetitive disappointment in self; the self feels powerless, defeated by its own addiction. Furthermore, the addiction functions by substituting sedation of intense negative affect for shame-bound interpersonal needs. Critical failures in the human environment have resulted in deep shame surrounding these vital human needs. The progression from sedative scripts to preaddictive scripts and then to addictive scripts is central to an understanding of the nature of addiction. Finally, affect hunger, affect promiscuity, and affect displacement are three additional affect dynamics that shape the addictive process.[51]

In the relationship that Kaufman establishes between shame and addictive disorders, there are two important points to note. First, there is a repetitive chain reaction: shame→addiction→more shame. At the beginning, this can be an unrecognized process even if, once the person feels addicted, such an awareness can generate conscious feelings of shame. Second, there is the importance of the role that addictions play as substitutions of "negative affect for shame-bound interpersonal needs."[52]

Carl Goldberg also studies the role of unrecognized or bypassed shame in the lives of his patients. He emphasizes:

Until quite recently clinicians' view of human behavior seriously neglected how people unknowingly shame themselves and the variety of ways that they allow others to humiliate them in their daily interactions. Shame is a cloaked emotion. Like an unseen powerful electric current, shame may cause a person serious harm without his being aware of its presence. An understanding of shame is complicated by the indirect consequences and the delays in responding to a shame stimulus.

I estimate that more than 90 percent of everyday experiences of being shamed lie buried beneath the surface of one's conscious awareness. During moments of being seriously shamed, the powerful hurt and the person's ability to identify the emotion that he is experiencing may be "bypassed."[53]

What is interesting in Goldberg's position is the recognition of the negative influences of unowned shame in daily social interactions. The harm people often inflict on each other in their relationships is caused, to a great extent, by bypassed shame.

Finally, Michael Lewis also elaborates on felt and unfelt shame, but he prefers to use the term *unowned* shame. This author considers that the position of Helen B. Lewis regarding shame "in the lives of people having real difficulties"[54] is too narrow, because it considers shame solely within the context of pathology. For him, shame is placed "within a more normal context . . . not from a pathological point of view but from an affective cognitive view."[55] According to my understanding, in contrast to Helen B. Lewis, Michael Lewis, among other authors, does not make any distinction between unacknowledged and bypassed shame. Thus, for our purposes, I use *unacknowledged shame, unidentified shame, unrecognized shame, unfelt shame, unowned shame* or *bypassed shame* synonymously.

As already affirmed by Goldberg, Michael Lewis also believes that a large percentage of people experience unacknowledged shame in their everyday interactions. Thus, according to the latter author, "Much of the effect of shame in our lives occurs because of unacknowledged shame. Indeed, it may well be the case that the major portion of shame within our lives is unacknowledged or bypassed."[56] Therefore, we can better understand that if on the one hand people experience shame in an unacknowledged way, and if, on the other hand, unowned shame produces pain in human interactions, then the harm that people do to each other because of unowned shame could be reduced considerably if they were able to own their own shame.

For M. Lewis, individuals deal with acknowledged shame through "forgetting, humor, and confession."[57] Nonetheless, the consequences of unowned shame are significant:

Unacknowledged, denied, repressed, or bypassed shame exerts its detrimental force in two ways within our intrapsychic life. The first has to do with the problem of not understanding what is happening in our lives, namely, that unacknowledged shame causes behavior that we cannot readily account for, and therefore leads us into trouble in terms of its effect. The second difficulty concerns the problem inherent in all strong emotions that are repressed or denied. It was Freud's original notion that repressed aspects of the psyche are not resolved, and this acts in a metaphorical sense as an irritant. The idea of repression leading to psychic irritation is in keeping with H. B. Lewis's idea distilled from traditional psychoanalysis: repressed events cause psychopathology.[58]

However, for M. Lewis, contrary to H. B. Lewis, "the problem with unacknowledged or bypassed shame is less that it is an irritant and more that it is unavailable as an explanation, for individuals attempting to account for their behavior either to themselves or to others with whom they interact."[59] According to M. Lewis, two emotions result from unowned shame: *sadness* and *anger*. Both produce symptoms that are similar to those of shame, namely, feeling bad, self-blame, pain, and so forth. Furthermore, sadness, anger and even rage, "which is uncontrolled anger,"[60] emerge in relationships with significant others.

For these reasons, Melvin R. Lansky accentuates the need to be attentive to bypassed shame in the therapeutic process.[61] Thus, the inability or the unwillingness to recognize toxic shame leads people to react to their feelings in inappropriate ways. They often consider their life a failure, avoid reference to important events, deny the facts that affect them, cover up or behave in a secretive way, feel embarrassed or humiliated, vulnerable, and powerless.

In summary, these situations can further degenerate into isolation, evasion, sadness, depression, self-contempt, low self-esteem, envy, rage, aggression, arrogance, sarcasm, blaming others, cynicism, abusiveness and manipulation in relationships, as well as perfectionism, grandiosity, dissociative identity disorders, and narcissistic personalities. The most negative consequence of chronic or dysfunctional shame, even when bypassed, is suicide.

From Shame to Suicide

There are two important ways in which suicide is related to shame. In the first case, the link between suicide and shame is direct, in that suicide is the act by which the person copes with excessive shame.[62] The second way is more subtle. In this case suicide is the result of unowned or bypassed shame. In the next chapter, I elaborate this "shame-suicide" connection, but here I wish to introduce its problem.

Although some societies consider suicide an honorable way of handling shame, I believe that suicide, as a result of undue shame, is a maladaptive way of dealing with these painful experiences, usually a response lacking in sufficient problem-solving skills. This is particularly the case in suicides of children and adolescents, but also of the elderly.[63]

Judith M. Stillion and Bethany D. Stillion have studied the direct link between suicide and shame in a historical perspective. According to them between 300 B.C. and 300 A.D., under the influence of stoic philosophy in Greece and Rome, "Suicide, in some instances, was considered to be a rational act that enabled a human to have control over the time and nature of his or her death."[64] Suicide was a dignified way of dying in ancient Greece.

The link between shame and suicide appears, too, in the work of Sophocles (495–405 B.C.). Lansky studied the role of shame in the suicide of Sophocles' *Ajax*. According to him, "Ajax's psychological vulnerability, his shame-proneness of which he becomes progressively more aware, is the tragic flaw which destines him for disgrace and inevitable suicide in a misguided and desperate attempt to restore his pathological pride."[65] Pathological pride, or hubris (arrogance), is a manifestation of bypassed shame.[66]

Some contemporary societies as, for example, Japan, also consider suicide an honorable way of dealing with shame. According to Jennifer Robertson, "Suicide is a key component of a Japanese national allegory."[67] Michael Lewis says that "In prewar Japan, shame was associated with suicide. Indeed, suicide was an expected and appropriate response to being shamed."[68] Nevertheless, suicide is not considered an acceptable way of dealing with excessive shame in today's Western society; rather, it is a dysfunctional means of coping with it.

Warren Breed did an empirical study regarding five components in the basic suicide syndrome in which he concluded that "Shame, the fourth component, is the suicider's *response to failure in a major role.*"[69] In this sense, the results of his study showed that the major trigger for suicide is *failure*, either as a result of "being fired, demoted, or passed over for promotion, or . . . suffer[ing] business reverses."[70] This feeling of failure occurs also in its relationship with hopelessness, particularly among adolescent suicides, another cause of suicide brought about by bypassed shame. The feeling that one's life is or has been a failure, with the added consequence of a sense of hopelessness, together with social isolation and depression, can also be one of the reasons for suicide in late adulthood.

Barry W. Shreve and Mark A. Kunkel studied the role of shame as a cause of suicide in adolescents. For these authors, suicide is "an extreme example of an attempt to escape from the pain of shame."[71] Consequently,

> suicidal thinking or behaviors may be considered manifestations of integral feelings of shame, "maladaptive" efforts to ameliorate the feelings of shame and prevent further deterioration of the sense of self, or as a last-ditch effort to defend against being overwhelmed by unwanted emotions. These processes can all occur simultaneously as well.[72]

Shame and Rage

For Lewis, "Suicide is likely to be the result of shame associated with rage directed inward. . . . As murder is the outward manifestation of the shame-rage spiral, suicide is its inward manifestation."[73] This is also the position of the Potter-Efrons for whom "severe combination of shame and anger also promote suicide. This combination produces people who think they are so worthless or bad that they must die."[74] Rage and anger, then, are also signs of bypassing shame.

Hartmut B. Mokros, too, establishes a direct relationship between shame and suicide. He bases his position on the analysis of the extracts of the audiotaped notes of two young men, Greg and Mark, who committed suicide. For the purposes of this analysis, Mokros followed the theory of human motivation proposed by Thomas J. Scheff and Suzanne M. Retzinger "that treats shame as central to an understanding of human action and experience."[75] In shame, the ego-ideal feels it has failed to achieve its own standards. There is then an objectification of the self, "within a ground of social expectations voiced by social others."[76] Therefore,

> The meaningful experience of the self when the shame experience runs amok is one of desperate preoccupation with one's identity, one's sense of place, within a milieu of deeply experienced, at times intolerable, psychic pain. Suicide provides one solution by which a person perceives the possibility of escape from this condition of the self.[77]

Analyzing what made Greg and Mark commit suicide, Mokros says: "Examination of each note, in its entirety, provides ample evidence of (a) a deeply humiliated state of being, (b) a failure to acknowledge this humiliation, and (c) an absence of someone to turn to, a lack of secure social bond."[78] In addition, Mokros indicates that Mark "exhibits continuous efforts to suppress his emotional experience through topic shifts, rationalization, and avoidance of manifest anger toward Dennis [his male lover]."[79] Consequently, in Mokros' position, escape from the self and the suppression of emotions are essential elements in the relationship between shame and suicide.

David Lester has systematically studied the role of shame in suicide. In his 1997 study, he analyzes the position of Mokros, but does not fully agree with the latter's view "that suicides motivated by shame involve the suppression of emotions."[80] Furthermore, "it is not convincing to view suicide simply as an escape from the self; it must also be an escape from the other."[81] However, this does not mean that Lester does not establish a relationship between shame and suicide. On the contrary, his position is that shame, for example among the unemployed, can degenerate into suicide. Therefore, the link between shame and suicide is, according to Lester, stronger in adolescents, among those that are in jails and detention facilities, and among those with various types of psychiatric pathology such as narcissistic personality disorders, borderline personality disorder, schizo-phrenia, depressive disorders or confusional states, and psychoses. Accordingly, an inadequate responsiveness from significant others, as in the case of children and adolescents, the shame generated by a jail sentence for minor offenses, the lack of constant attention from others, in the case of narcissistic people, the shame of being neglected, in the case of those with borderline personality disorder, and the shame experienced after a particular recovery, by those who suffer from schizo-phrenia, depressive disorders or confusional states, may lead to suicide.

Recently other researchers have dealt with the relationship between manifested or bypassed shame and suicide.[82] The main conclusion we can draw from their research is that suicide is the result of a lack of problem-solving skills for dealing with stressful experiences, such as shame, usually bypassed. This lack of skills is particularly evident in adolescents.

Shame and Hopelessness

Currently, "the most robust and consistent of predictors and correlates of suicidality across all age groups is hopelessness."[83] Bypassed shame also plays an influential role in hopelessness and is referred to as *existential shame* or the feeling of worth-lessness. "This is the kind of shame that most often leaves people feeling hopeless about the meaning of their lives and that most predicts suicidality."[84]

Finally, the connection between bypassed shame and suicide is mostly an inferred one. Melvin Lansky directly links unowned shame and suicide: "Shame, however, is usually masked or hidden behind depression, guilt, psychic pain, anger or anxiety-ridden states of turbulence."[85] This can also be considered the position of Shreve and Kunkel, who accentuate in their study the relationship between shame and suicide in adolescents:

> When either chronic or traumatic injuries occur to the already fragile self, the person becomes shamed in his or her own eyes and may then use strategies such as substance abuse, delinquency, or suicide to escape the pain and thereby prevent further deteriora-tion of the sense of self.[86]

The relationship between bypassed shame and suicide in children and ado-lescents can also be deduced from the study of Mauri J. Marttunen, Hillevi M. Aro, and Jouko K. Lönnqvist.[87] According to them, humiliating events, such as physical and sexual abuse, in themselves already sources of shame, may actually bring about suicide among children and adolescents.

Mokros, too, has studied the role of unacknowledged shame in suicide, a posi-tion that will be developed further in the next chapter. In particular, he highlights the negative effects, suicide being the most lethal, of the absence of a social place for shame-prone people.[88]

The connection between bypassed shame and suicide can also be found in the link between perfectionism and suicide. Perfectionism, in its pathological connotation, is closely related to narcissism. Perfectionism and narcissism, as we will see in the next chapter, are inadequate ways of attempting to avoid the shame and humiliation of falling below certain unrealistic standards set by the ego-ideal. The link between *perfectionism* and suicide is well documented in the literature regarding the motives for suicide.

Consequently, in their study, John Kalafat and David Lester refer to the special attention that therapists must pay to bypassed shame while working with suicidal clients. "Shame seeks secrecy, and a failure to notice the client's shame may result in 'unexpected' suicidal behavior."[89] It is extremely important to have a better understanding of the role of shame in people's lives.

Conclusion

This chapter has dealt with the role that shame plays in human development. In order to understand this role, it was necessary first to recognize the multiple expressions of shame and second to recognize how shame can be unowned or bypassed. Finally, the chapter has presented the ways in which shame, directly or bypassed, leads to suicide. We need to acquire a better understanding of the role that shame plays in human development in order to overcome its negative consequences in people's lives.

I find this dynamic of becoming familiar with the different influences of shame in our lives, with its multiple manifestations and connections, extremely important for acquiring a healthier personality and for living a more fulfilled life. First, the simple fact of understanding some of the significant experiences that had a negative influence in our lives initiates a process of freedom. Second, it is important not only to identify these painful events, but also to own these maladaptive characteristics of shame in our development. In this way we can overcome its negative influences. Owning these experiences of our lives is a way of giving them a voice so that we may better understand what they are trying to tell us. Finally, it liberates us from being ashamed of sharing these experiences with others, particularly with significant others.

The following chapter will elaborate in greater detail the place of unowned or bypassed shame in suicide.

Notes

1. Fossum & Mason, 1986.
2. Kaufman,1989, p. 4.
3. Fossum & Mason, 1986, p. ix.
4. Potter-Efron & Potter-Efron, 1999, p. 18.
5. Kaufman, 1989, p. 4.
6. Gramzow & Tangney, 1992; Hockenberry, 1995; Lewis, 1992; Mattox & Peck, 1992; Nathanson, 1992; Potter-Efron & Potter-Efron, 1999.
7. Bradshaw, 1988; Fossum & Mason, 1986; Gramzow & Tangney, 1992; Hockenberry, 1995; Jacoby, 1994; Mattox & Peck, 1992; Nathanson, 1992.
8. Goldberg, 1991, p. 55.
9. Lewis, 1987a, p. 18. Italics in the original text.
10. Lewis, 1987b, p. 29.
11. Pattison, 2000, pp. 96–97.
12. Lewis, 1992, p. 138.
13. Lewis, 1992, p. 9.
14. Lewis, 1992, p. 75.
15. Lewis, 1992, p. 91.
16. Breed, 1972, pp. 7–8.
17. Gaulejac, 1996; Jacoby, 1994; Pattison, 2000; Rizzuto, 1991.
18. Lewis, 1987a, p. 3.
19. Bradshaw, 1988, p. vii.
20. Nathanson, 1992; Pattison, 2000.
21. Bradshaw, 1988; Lewis, 1987a.
22. Pattison, 2000, p. 84.
23. Goldberg, 1991; Potter-Efron & Potter-Efron, 1999.
24. Pattison, 2000, p. 181.
25. Lewis, 1992, p. 34.
26. Goldberg, 1991, p. 25.
27. Pattison, 2000, p. 108.
28. Nathanson, 1992, p. 135.
29. Lewis, 1992, p. 1.
30. Rizzuto, 1991, p. 298.
31. Rizzuto, 1991, p. 304. Italics in the original text.
32. Fossum & Mason, 1986.
33. Kaufman, 1989, p. 4.
34. Kaufman, 1989; Potter-Efron & Potter-Efron, 1999.
35. Nathanson, 1992; Pattison, 2000.
36. Halling, 1994, p. 79.
37. Ikonen & Rechardt, 1993, p. 100.

38   Bradshaw, 1988; Frølund, 1997; Gaulejac, 1996; Goldberg, 1991; Hahn, 2000; Harper & Hoopes, 1990; Kaufman, 1989; Lansky, 1996; Lewis, 1992; Pattison, 2000; Rizzuto, 1991; Tisseron, 1992.
39   Lewis, 1987a, p. 19.
40   Bradshaw, 1988, p. 58.
41   Pattison, 2000, p. 131.
42   Chance, 1992; Gaulejac, 1996; Gyulay, 1989; Knieper, 1999; Pattison, 2000; Potter-Efron & Potter-Efron, 1999.
43   Bradshaw, 1988, p. 73.
44   Pattison, 2000, p. 156.
45   Goldberg, 1991, pp. xvi–xvii.
46   Harper & Hoopes, 1990, p. 171.
47   Halling, 1994; Lewis, 1992; Mattox & Peck, 1992.
48   Gaulejac, 1996; Gyulay, 1989.
49   Pattison, 2000, p. 155.
50   Lewis, 1987a, pp. 22–23.
51   Kaufman, 1989, pp. 132–133.
52   Kaufman, 1989, p. 132.
53   Goldberg, 1991, p. 15.
54   Lewis, 1992, p. 120.
55   Lewis, 1992, p. 120.
56   Lewis, 1992, p. 120.
57   Lewis, 1992, p. 120.
58   Lewis, 1992, p. 120.
59   Lewis, 1992, p. 120.
60   Pattison, 2000, p. 127.
61   Lansky, 1991.
62   Pattison, 2000.
63   Goldston et al., 2001.
64   Stillion & Stillion, 1998–99, p. 78.
65   Lansky, 1996, p. 767.
66   Lewis, 1992; Nathanson, 1992; Potter-Efron & Potter-Efron, 1999.
67   Robertson, 1999, p. 12.
68   Lewis, 1992, p. 161.
69   Breed, 1972, p. 7. Italics in the original text.
70   Breed, 1972, p. 6.
71   Shreve & Kunkel, 1991, p. 307.
72   Shreve & Kunkel, 1991, p. 309.
73   Lewis, 1992, p. 161.
74   Potter-Efron & Potter-Efron, 1999, p. 194.
75   Mokros, 1995, p. 1091.

[76]   Mokros, 1995, p. 1095.

[77]   Mokros, 1995, p. 1096.

[78]   Mokros, 1995, p. 1097.

[79]   Mokros, 1995, p. 1098.

[80]   Lester, 1997, p. 354.

[81]   Lester, 1997, p. 354.

[82]   Beautrais, 2000; McClelland et al., 2000; Stanard, 2000; Westefeld et al., 2000.

[83]   Stanard, 2000, p. 206.

[84]   Potter-Efron & Potter-Efron, 1999, p. 42.

[85]   Lansky, 1991, p. 232.

[86]   Shreve & Kunkel, 1991, p. 308.

[87]   Marttunen, Aro, & Lönnqvist, 1993.

[88]   Mokros, 1995.

[89]   Kalafat & Lester, 2000, p. 161.

Chapter II

Pictures of Shame in Suicide

This second chapter will deal with what I have found to be the most important current models for understanding shame insofar as it has a bearing on suicide. I would like to begin by highlighting four points made in the previous chapter. The first is the frequency with which one has to infer the presence of chronic shame from its effects on people's lives. Thus, Goldberg, Kaufman, H. B. Lewis, M. Lewis, Nathanson, and Pattison have pointed out the negative influence of unowned or bypassed shame in personal and social interactions. One of these consequences is precisely that the person does not know what is happening to himself or herself, being unable to recognize his or her emotions as dysfunctional expressions of shame. The second point, following Lansky, is the importance of the recognition of unacknowledged or bypassed shame in therapy in order to avoid the previous risk, that is, an inappropriate reaction to one's feelings. The third point is the fact that suicide can also be a result of unrecognized shame. This point has been clearly shown recently by Kalafat and Lester.[1] Finally, suicide is often the result of a lack of problem-solving skills, particularly among adolescents and the elderly, for dealing with stressful experiences.

Taking into account what Lansky suggested regarding the need for discerning the danger of bypassed shame in therapy, in this chapter I shall accentuate the necessity of such discernment. This necessity is due not only to its importance in the therapeutic process but also to its importance for anyone interested in the topic of shame and suicide. Accordingly, it is essential to identify some forms of behavior through which shame manifests itself, such as alienation from oneself and from others, or hopelessness, depression and alcoholism, or again perfectionism and narcissism. These behaviors are often intimately connected to suicide.

The first part of this chapter deals with how alienation from oneself and from others can be present in both shame and suicide. This link is important. The isolation, the desire to hide from others, and so forth, which are attitudes typical of a shame-prone personality, can also be indicators of something more grave, namely, suicidal behavior.

Second, the chapter analyzes the progression towards hopelessness→ depression→alcoholism→suicide. Hopelessness is one of the most important components in depression. However, depression can also be one of the reasons for alcoholism, and they all can be bypassed manifestations of shame. In addition, hopelessness, depression and alcoholism are among the most common triggers for suicidal behavior. This maladaptive connection, hopelessness→depression→alcoholism (substance abuse)→suicide, is especially common in suicidal behavior among adolescents and the elderly.

Third, this chapter spells out the relationship between perfectionism, narcissism and suicide. Perfectionism and narcissism are closely related. As such, they are not necessarily maladaptive dimensions of a person. One could try to perform or to excel without having the pathological dimension that perfectionism takes on in some people. Besides, according to some psychological theories, narcissism plays an important role in the early stages of life. Nevertheless, narcissism, like perfectionism, can become pathological when, for example, it becomes a manifestation of unowned or bypassed shame. Consequently, persons can try to hide their lack of self-esteem through perfectionism or by considering themselves the center of the universe in a narcissistic way. In any case, suicide can be the final and most extreme act of overcoming the painful events of these dysfunctional personalities.

Alienation from Self, Alienation from Others

Usually shame-prone people experience alienation and separateness not only from others but also from themselves. They have the tendency to hide or to disappear from others.[2] One of the reasons for withdrawing from social interaction is the lack of self-esteem and the belief that one does not deserve to be loved by others. What is more, as Bradshaw indicates, the person who lives alienated from himself or herself develops "a false identity."[3] Suicide can be the ultimate expression of the alienated self.

Following a chronological approach to the relationship between social isolation and suicide, I would like to cite Warren Breed who, speaking about five components of the basic suicide syndrome, emphasizes the importance that *social isolation* has in relation to suicide. When the need of every human being to be validated and socially recognized by others is taken into account, the absence of adequate support can have deadly consequences:

> The suicider anticipates this kind of evaluation from others, feeling that the stigmata of failure and self-exposure are visible to all. He "takes the role of the other," and in such a situation social gratification and mutuality become less likely for the other person as well as for the suicider. Old contacts atrophy, and new ones are avoided. This may help

to explain why suicide is only infrequently an impulse act; it takes time for the person to perceive "labeling" from others.[4]

For Breed, the link between shame and suicide through personal and social isolation is quite evident. As indicated in Chapter I, a person who considers himself or herself a failure may view suicide as the way to overcome feelings of shame in the face of an anticipated reaction from others. What is more, suicide is the outcome of a long process rather than the consequence of one impulsive act in the face of some negative circumstances.

This relationship between alienation from the self and others and suicide is also corroborated by the *escape theory* of suicide. Here, suicide is a way of escaping aversive self-awareness. Roy F. Baumeister stresses that suicide can be seen as the ultimate step in an effort to escape from the self and the world. According to him,

> There are six main steps in the escape theory. First, a severe experience that current outcomes (or circumstances) fall far below standards is produced either by unrealistically high expectations or by recent problems or setbacks, or by both. Second, internal attributions are made, so that these disappointing outcomes are blamed on the self and create negative implications about the self. Third, an aversive state of high self-awareness comes from comparing the self with relevant standards (in connection with self-blame for recent disappointments). The individual is thus acutely aware of self as inadequate, incompetent, unattractive, or guilty. Fourth, negative affect arises from the unfavorable comparison of self with standards. Fifth, the person responds to this unhappy state by trying to escape from meaningful thought into a relatively numb state of cognitive deconstruction. This escape is not fully successful, however, and so the individual desires increasingly stronger means of terminating the aversive thoughts and feelings. Sixth, the consequences of this deconstructed mental state include a reduction of inhibitions, which may contribute to an increased willingness to attempt suicide. Suicide thus emerges as an escalation of the person's wish to escape from meaningful awareness of current life problems and their implications about the self.[5]

Here we are in the presence of someone who compares herself or himself with unrealistic standards. She or he makes global attributions to the self, considering the self basically bad, or feeling unworthy of being respected by others. For Baumeister, "There is a fair amount of evidence linking suicide with negative views of the self."[6] Suicide, then, can be the ultimate way of dealing with aversive experiences. Nonetheless, the tendency to escape from painful experiences regarding oneself, such as the one described by Baumeister, and by Breed before him, is also a manifestation of shame even in an unowned or bypassed way.

This escapist way of dealing with painful experiences is particularly present in adolescent suicides. In this important sector of the population, suicide is, according to Gary W. Mauk and Claudia Weber, the result of a lack of coping mechanisms. Thus, "adolescents can turn to escapist measures such as drugs, which further distance them from reality and later lead them to view suicide as the 'only way out.' "[7] Moreover, these authors add that "Suicide in adolescents can be briefly described as a result of increasing alienation from society combined with a decrease in coping skills and inadequate socialization of young people to adulthood."[8]

Melvin Lansky directly connects shame with suicide from a family systems perspective. For him, shame is the result of a failure in human attachments and an indicator of a narcissistic wounding as a consequence of this failure. In this sense, personal and social isolation, which can lead the person to commit suicide, is the final outcome of the inability to establish healthy attachments:

> The view of the suicidal patient from a family systems perspective is that of a person whose significant bonds to intimates have either become acutely jeopardised or exposed as chronically doomed to failure, for example, because of repeated losses of control, over-whelming self-absorption caused by unremitting psychiatric illness, or habitually intimidating styles of relating by threats of suicide or violence. The final common pathways of these predicaments is a *threatened awareness of loss of the capacity for intimate bondings due to defects in the self*, i.e. to shame and the exposure of a self that has a pre-existing sense of shame hitherto buried in intimate relationships but now threatened with exposure.[9]

Shame and Cognitive Distortions

Frequently, continues Lansky, the isolation from others and finally from oneself is the result of a personal cognitive distortion of the situation rather than really being rooted in the attitudes of others toward the person. This behavioral characteristic marking some people is the consequence of shame, and shame can lead to suicide:

> The assumption is often made that other prominent affects or emotional states are central to the suicidal predicament. Depression, guilt, psychic pain and anger have all been considered to be primary sources of suicidal anguish. I shall argue that these emotional states play a secondary role in the suicidal patient and that the primary emotional mortification is due to shame. Shame, however, is usually masked or hidden behind depression, guilt, psychic pain, anger or anxiety-ridden states of turbulence.[10]

Separation from significant others, then, and alienation from oneself are particularly present in suicide among adolescents. One of the reasons for this, as already indicated, is the lack of coping mechanisms for dealing with painful situations. Marttunen et al., discussing the result of their empirical research regarding precipitant stressors in adolescent (aged 13 to 19 years) suicides, stress that

> The finding that interpersonal separations were common precipitants especially in the context of weakened support from parents emphasizes the importance of assessing sources of social support. The adolescent's history of separations, family history, and current

family situation should be evaluated. When the suicidal adolescent cannot find enough support from family members, extrafamilial supportive network should be provided.[11]

It is important to emphasize here, even taking into account that the connection between shame, suicide and bereavement will be presented and analyzed later in the fourth chapter, that suicide, as a result of alienation from oneself and others, can be a real threat for people grieving deaths by suicide. Martti Heikkinen, Hillevi Aro, and Jouko Lönnqvist indicate that "There is evidence that bereavement increases the suicide risk during the following years, especially among males. . . . Unmarried men especially seemed to be at high risk for suicide in the period following their mothers' death."[12]

One of the reasons for this behavior is the loss that the bereaved person is experiencing. Such a loss can lead to other psychological vulnerabilities, such as alienation from oneself and from others, hopelessness, depression, alcoholism or other substance abuse and, finally, suicide.[13]

Hartmut B. Mokros, following Baumeister, presents the connection between shame and suicide, and highlights how breaking out of social bonds, with the result of personal and social isolation, leads to suicide as a way of escaping from the experience of excessive shame:

> The link of shame to suicide requires that we consider how this normative regulatory function of shame becomes dysfunctional such that the individual experiences "no sense of social place." This occurs when shame is "unacknowledged," as it is either masked or bypassed altogether and becomes internalized and generative of its own production. Typically these "feeling traps" (Scheff, 1990) involve a cycling between states of shame and anger, or what Lewis (1971) called "humiliated fury." In cycling between shame and anger, concern with identity becomes thematically focal. In shame there is the experience of rejection from the social bond, and in anger, the experience of rejecting one's place in the social bond.[14]

Isolation from oneself and from others is also one of the "Major predictors of suicidal behaviour"[15] not only among adolescents, but also for the elderly. Adolescents and the elderly, as I have indicated in the Introduction to the present study, are the two sectors of the population with the major number of suicide attempts.

My remarks regarding alienation from oneself and from others, which results from chronic shame and which can lead to suicide, should make us pay more attention to people with a low degree of socialization. Annette Beautrais underlines this point in a paper in which she summarizes current knowledge about risk factors for suicide attempts in young people in Australia and New Zealand since the mid-1980s. Social inadequacy is one of the personality factors that, according to her, can predispose to suicide. There is no doubt that alienation from oneself and from others is an inappropriate way of dealing with painful experiences. Regarding alienation from oneself and others, Beautrais is one of the researchers who point out the particular risk to which gay, lesbian and bisexual people seem to be susceptible, particularly among the younger segments of the population: "Specifically, it has been argued that, because of a series of social processes centering around homophobic attitudes, gay, lesbian and bisexual youth are exposed to serious social and personal stresses that increase their likelihood of suicidal behaviour."[16] I can personally corroborate what she says regarding this last point. During my years growing up in the south of Spain, I saw how my culture of origin, along with many others, reflected homophobic attitudes. Those who were gay, lesbian or bisexual had to live in social isolation, ashamed, stigmatized, and prone to suicide. They questioned themselves about their own sexual orientation and, as a result, frequently became alienated from their own selves.

Finally, Apter et al. also accentuate the relationship between alienation or isolation and suicide. The inability to disclose oneself to others, which is at the center of social isolation, can lead to suicidal behavior. In discussing the results of their study of the relationship between self-disclosure and serious suicidal behavior in patients hospitalized with affective disorders, Apter et al. write:

> Our hypothesis that self-disclosure is limited in subjects with more severe suicidal behavior than in subjects with milder suicidal behavior was to a large extent supported by our results. In addition, self-disclosure appears to be independent of the degree of depression/anxiety and hopelessness. Thus, it may be that limited self-disclosure acts as a mediating risk factor that facilitates serious suicidal behavior when other risk factors such as psychopathology, anxiety/depression, and hopelessness are present.[17]

Consequently, an incapacity for self-disclosure, which is common among shame-prone personalities, leads people to feel isolated and alone, increasing the risk of suicide. Alienation from oneself and from others can also be the cause or the consequence of hopelessness, depression, and alcoholism.

Hopelessness, Depression, Alcoholism, Suicide

Another way of recognizing unowned or bypassed shame is by noting the presence of a sense of hopelessness. However, even if we recognize that there is a connection between shame and depression, and between shame and alcoholism or substance abuse in general, and without necessarily relating them to hopelessness, it seems important to stress the fact that a sequence can often be established. Hopelessness is like the activator, the initiating process, that can lead to depression. Hopelessness and depression play an essential role in substance abuse and addictions. Hopelessness and depression, together with alcoholism, have a major influence on suicidal behavior. I describe in this second section the link among hopelessness→depression→alcoholism→suicide.

Aaron T. Beck is one of the leading and most cited of the psychologists studying the connection between hopelessness, depression, alcoholism and suicide. For him thoughts of *escaping* from difficult situations are the result of important cognitive distortions of reality and have an enormous influence on suicide. The desire to escape from painful experiences is related to the suicidal person's belief that he or she is in a hopeless situation. Suicide then appears as the only possible solution:

> The suicidal wishes may be regarded as an extreme expression of the desire to escape. The suicidal patient sees his future as filled with suffering. He cannot visualize any way of improving things. He does not believe it is possible to get better. Suicide under these conditions seems to the patient to be a rational solution. It promises an end to his own suffering and a relief of the supposed burden on his family. Once suicide appears as a reasonable alternative to living, the patient feels attracted to it. The more hopeless and painful his life seems, the stronger his desire to escape from that life.[18]

According to Beck's 1967 publication, *Depression: Clinical, Experimental, and Theoretical Aspects,* the link between hopelessness or depression and suicide is essential. Hopelessness, negative expectations, and a pessimistic view of the future are some of the most important specific factors rendering one vulnerable to depression. Therefore, "When these attitudes are mobilized they produce the feeling of hopelessness characteristic of depression."[19]

That relationship has often been verified. In an overview of hopelessness and suicidal behaviors, Beck et al. explore the theory that suicidal behavior is the consequence of a cognitive distortion of reality and hopelessness is a "catalytic agent."[20] That is, "The main thrust of Beck's argument is that the suicidal behavior of the depressed patient is derived from specific cognitive distortions: the patient systematically misconstrues his experiences in a negative way and, without objective basis, anticipates a negative outcome to any attempts to attain his major objectives or goals."[21] The fact that hopelessness, in its connection to depression, is the most important indicator of suicidal behavior must alert clinicians to this reality: "By focusing on reduction of a patient's hopelessness, the professional may also be able to alleviate suicidal crises more effectively than in the past."[22]

Since Aaron T. Beck, the role of hopelessness as a trigger for suicide and suicidal ideation has been well-documented. I would like to present here, in chronological order, some of the most significant dimensions of this research.

J. Mark G. Williams and Leslie R. Pollock, in their research of British and American studies regarding the factors mediating suicidal behavior and their utility in primary and secondary prevention, point out the central role that hopelessness frequently plays as a mediation between depression and suicide. Hopelessness has a role in the repetition of the parasuicidal act or in suicide completed after several years of attempting. Like Beck, Williams and Pollock emphasize the importance of hopelessness as the result of a distorted cognitive process regarding the possibilities for the future, even the immediate future. They also bring out the relationship they see among hopelessness, depression and suicide. Williams and Pollock conclude that one needs to pay attention to the symptoms of depression in order to forestall the ultimate act of suicide.[23]

In the already cited empirical research done by Marttunen et al., the relationship between depression, substance abuse and suicide was shown to be strongly present among suicidal people. This was established by using psychological autopsy methods based on interviews with family members and other people related to adolescents who had committed suicide.

Tracey E. Harry and Christ J. Lennings conducted research at the Westbrook Youth Training Centre (Australia) involving forty-seven young male volunteers aged 15 to 19 years (mean age = 16) regarding the role that family background, substance abuse, depression, and hopelessness may have in suicidal behavior. Contrary to the tendency to emphasize the important role of hopelessness as a triggering factor for suicide, they arrived at the following conclusion:

> This study suggests that depression is a major predictor of suicide risk. Unlike other research that has indicated that depression combined with hopelessness is a major factor in predicting suicide, the current study found no evidence to hold that hopelessness plays an important mediating role in the prediction of suicidal ideation or attempts.[24]

In fact, there is no doubt that depression, either bipolar (depression accompanied by alternating periods of mania, and for this reason also called manic-depressive disorder) or unipolar (depression without mania), has a very negative influence in relation to suicide. According to Rosenhan and Seligman,

> Depressed individuals are the single group most at risk for suicide. While suicide occasionally occurs in the absence of depression and the large majority of depressed people do not commit suicide, depression is a strong predisposing factor to suicide. An estimated 80 percent of suicidal patients are significantly depressed. Depressed patients ultimately commit suicide at a rate that is as least twenty-five times as high as control populations.[25]

Depression and Suicide

Nevertheless, the majority of the research analyzed indicates a link between hopelessness and depression: not only does hopelessness play a major role in suicide and suicidal ideation, it is also a determinant factor in depression.

The influence of hopelessness, depression and alcoholism on suicide is also highlighted by Paula I. Clayton. Referring to psychological autopsies, Clayton says that depression, together with alcoholism, is "particularly lethal"[26] among people with panic disorders. However, according to her, "The symptom that correlates most clearly and repeatedly with an outcome of suicide is hopelessness."[27]

Matt Stoelb and Jennifer Chiriboga, working out a process model for assessing adolescents' risk for suicide, also underline how hopelessness is one of the primary risk factors in adolescent suicide. They consider substance abuse to be a secondary risk factor and life stressors to be situational risk factors. "Examples of adolescent stressors include disciplinary actions taken against the adolescent, incidences of rejection and/or humiliation [*sic*] by others, moves to new environments, terminations of friendships or relationships, and arguments with relatives or friends."[28] In this sense, Kaplan et al., analyzing the literature dealing with adolescent physical abuse and risk for suicidal behavior, point out that apart from the connection between hopelessness, depression and suicide,

> the literature indicates that victims of physical abuse are more likely to be exposed to additional risk factors for suicidal behavior such as parental and adolescent depression (as well as other forms of adolescent psychopathology), lack of family and peer support, and poor academic functioning. In the present study of physically abused adolescents, each of these risk factors was found to predict at least one type of behavior related to increased suicide risk.[29]

For their part, Karyn Gust-Brey and Tracy Cross,[30] examining the literature based on the suicidal behaviors of gifted students, also found that suicide is closely linked to hopelessness and depression. This is valid, as Joan Klinger points out, not only for gifted students and adolescents in general but also for the elderly. She recognizes that, besides hopelessness and depression, loneliness appears to be "the major reason for considering suicide"[31] among American seniors.

From empirical research regarding suicide risk-assessment in a college student population at a Midwestern university in which a group of 211 students completed several questionnaires concerning suicide, Gutierrez, Osman, Kopper, Barrios, and Bagge identify several factors contributing to suicidal thoughts and behavior. Among the most important are "loneliness, hopelessness, depression, relationship problems, helplessness, academic problems, difficulties with parents, and financial concerns."[32] In line with previous research, they consider the importance of suicide risk assessment as a preventive measure to be essential, as other research does. According to them, "Early identification of those students at greatest risk would result in better use of intervention resources and could potentially decrease these individuals' lifetime risk."[33] In fact, the majority of the research done recently on suicide discusses the question of prevention in one way or another.

For Fritsch et al., hopelessness is the most important indicator for suicide in adults and adolescents. Following the finding of Beck and his many collaborators, they say:

> Beck et al. identified hopelessness in adults to be the best predictor of eventual completed suicide in a follow-up study of adults originally admitted for suicidal ideation. Adolescent studies have demonstrated that hopelessness is more strongly related to suicidal behavior than other behaviors or emotions, and that hospitalized adolescent suicide attempters have higher levels of hopelessness when compared to nonsuicidal psychiatrically hospitalized controls and normal controls.[34]

Westefeld et al., summarizing the factors which contribute to suicide, argue that

> suicidal individuals, compared with their nonsuicidal peers, have personalities that are more disturbed; affect that is more depressed and anxious; cognitions that are more negative; environments that are more adverse; and patterns of substance use and abuse that will depress them, lower their inhibitions, and impair their judgment. They suffer from hopelessness and helplessness, depression, anxiety disorders, and schizophrenia and are lonely, isolated, and physically ill to a greater extent than nonsuicidal individuals. They have histories of previous suicidal behaviors that increase their risk for future suicide and further distinguish them from their nonsuicidal peers. They will probably not communicate to others that they are suicidal.[35]

This summary describes very well the most important dimensions of suicide and suicidal behavior that have been presented thus far.

Apter et al. also accentuate the importance of hopelessness, depression and anxiety leading to suicidal behavior.[36] The association between hopelessness, depression and suicide is also indicated by the research of Goldston et al.,[37] and the survey done by Susan R. Furr, Gaye N. McConnel, John S. Westefeld, and J. Marshall Jenkins among 1,455 college students at four different colleges and universities. According to this survey, "Hopelessness was cited most frequently (49%) as a contributing factor to suicidal ideation or behavior by those students who identified themselves as having suicidal thoughts."[38] This is also the case with the elderly, for whom the relationship between hopelessness and depression is a major contributor for suicidal behavior. According to Van Ness and Larson, "Depression and, to a lesser extent, hopelessness, are established risk factors for suicide among elderly persons. They are also associated with desires for hastened death and suicidal ideation."[39] This risk increases during the process of grieving in old age.[40] In conclusion, following Holden and Kroner, it can be said that, "To date, hopelessness, defined as negative cognitions about the future, has emerged as the pre-eminent psychological antecedent of suicide and its various manifestations. . . . Further, in the statistical prediction of suicide manifestations, indices of hopelessness tend to be relatively more important than measures of depression."[41]

Substance Abuse

Alcoholism, like any other form of substance abuse, has a decisive influence on the relationship being presented here between hopelessness, depression and suicide. The link between alcoholism and suicidal behavior is one of the most studied in psychological research. When used in small or moderate amounts, alcohol can have a sedative effect and can counteract the negative mood arising in painful experiences. We should nevertheless note that "There is rather convincing evidence that alcohol use is often motivated by a desire to escape from self-awareness."[42] According to Hufford,

> the odds of mood improvement appear to diminish with increasing levels of intoxication and during periods of active alcohol dependence. Several studies have found that both attempted and completed suicides are more likely to occur during periods of heavy drinking characterized by increased depression (Black et al., 1986; Mayfield & Montgomery, 1972). These data provide support for the connection between alcohol intoxication, increased negative emotions, and suicidal behavior.[43]

A high level of intoxication impairs the cognitive functions of a person and increases the risk factor for suicide. Thus, "Possible mechanisms responsible for alcohol intoxication increasing the proximal risk of suicidal behavior include increased psychological distress, increased aggressiveness, suicide-specific alcohol expectancies, and cognitive constriction which impairs the generation and implementation of alternative coping strategies."[44] Alcoholism sets in motion a repetition of the cycle of alcoholism→shame→hopelessness→depression→intoxication→cognitive constrictions→impairment of coping strategies→suicide. For Alec Roy, "The suicide risk among alcoholics is at least twice that among the general population, and is 60 to 120 times higher than that of the nonpsychiatrically ill in the general population. Studies of suicide victims in the general population show that about 20 percent of such suicide victims are alcoholic."[45] According to Roy, the link between alcoholism and suicide is stronger among "Alcoholics with comorbid depressive disorders. . . ."[46] Moreover, "It has been suggested that alcohol abuse may be a depressive equivalent; that is, a person may turn to alcohol as a form of self-medication to escape from depression. On the other hand, chronic alcohol abuse may lead to depression."[47] Nevertheless, one needs to take into consideration what Danuta Wasserman indicates regarding the relationship between depression, alcoholism and suicide:

One problem with regard to suicidal alcoholics is that their depressions are often atypical and therefore difficult to recognize, since they arise against the background of a personality disorder and do not assume the characteristic features to which we are accustomed. Moreover, some alcoholics react with intensified depression or dysphoria during a period of abuse, which may reflect a toxic reaction.[48]

Wasserman describes the fact that alcoholism, in its association with mental disturbances, increases the risk of suicide. In a particular way, Roy emphasizes what has been manifested above, that is, that childhood traumas such as "emotional abuse, physical abuse, sexual abuse, emotional neglect, and physical neglect"[49] are important determinants for suicide among alcoholics. According to him, "This is noteworthy as recent studies report significant relationships between childhood trauma and both major depression and personality disorder as an adult, two common comorbidities in alcoholics which are also associated with suicidal behavior."[50] These findings on violence, physical or sexual abuse of children and adolescents, are well documented in the current literature regarding suicide.[51] In our Western culture, particularly in North American society, physical and sexual abuse of children and adolescents has become a real concern. If we take into account that these destructive abuses perpetrated on them frequently have lethal consequences, or will become possible factors for committing suicide, or will lead to suicidal behavior later on, we see that society has an important role to play in the prevention of all kinds of violence committed against anyone, but particularly against children and adolescents.

So far the present chapter has dealt with the destructive role arising from alienation from oneself and from others. I examined the relationship among hopelessness, depression and alcoholism as manifestations of unowned or bypassed shame in suicide and suicidal behavior. I wish now to show how shame also manifests its influence through perfectionism and narcissism, both of which are possible triggers for suicide.

Perfectionism, Narcissism, and Self Destruction

The relationship between perfectionism and narcissism, as unowned or bypassed manifestations of shame, and suicidal behavior is very important. There is a notion of perfectionism that is not necessarily maladaptive and neurotic. In this sense, people feel comfortable trying to do their best, to excel, but without becoming unhealthy, that is, without excelling or performing at any cost. Nevertheless, in its pathological manifestation, perfectionism can be defined "as the need to be first, best, perfect, and without shortcomings, blemishes, or deficiencies,"[52] and to do it at any cost. According to authors who describe some of the personality traits underlying perfectionism, "Common sense, self-esteem, self-confidence, courage, adequacy, social interest, and social skills are either deficient or absent."[53] As such, in its pathological dimension, perfectionism can be a way of compensating and hiding a sense of inferiority[54] and, as mentioned above, an indication of unowned or bypassed shame.

Suicide may become the ultimate act through which shame-prone personalities deliver themselves from this maladaptive tendency to perfectionism, when they realize the impossibility of keeping their feelings of inferiority and shame hidden. Furthermore, suicidal behavior can be a way of avoiding the feelings of shame that may result from the impossibility of always being the first or the best. This last tendency was often present, according to Karyn Gust-Brey and Tracy Cross, in the research cited above regarding the suicidal behavior of gifted students. That is, "individuals who are passive perfectionists are at-risk for attempting suicide. Passive perfectionists are individuals for whom perfectionism creates impediments, fear of making mistakes, and procrastination."[55] Therefore, in dealing with the problem of adolescent suicide attempts, one needs to assess and to pay close attention to the perfectionism traits of personality that some adolescents exhibit if we wish to help them to avoid the risk of suicidal behavior.

Interestingly, contrary to the normal role that some theorists think narcissism plays during the first steps of the lifespan, what makes it a personality disorder

> is an outlandish sense of self-importance. It is characterized by continuous self-absorption, by fantasies of unlimited success, power and/or beauty, by exhibitionistic needs for constant admiration, and by the use of a substantially more benign standard for evaluating self than for judging others. . . . Criticism, the indifference of others, and threats to esteem characteristically receive exaggerated responses of rage, shame, humiliation, or emptiness. Of course, the near-total preoccupation with self massively disturbs interpersonal relationships in a variety of ways. Such people may simply lack the ability to recognize how others feel. They may have an exaggerated sense of "entitlement," expecting that the world owes them a living without assuming reciprocal responsibilities. They may simply be exploitative, taking advantage of others to indulge their own desires. When they are able to establish a relationship, they may vacillate between the extremes of overidealization and enormous devaluation of the other person.[56]

Some suggest that it is parental training that makes children grow up expecting too much from others. Other psychologists believe that narcissism is the result of a failure of empathic relationships with significant others in the life of the infant which affects the hoped for development of the self in an integrated way. This fragmentation of the self engenders a person who "is especially vulnerable to feelings of emptiness and low self-esteem, and the compensatory behaviors that these generate."[57] Healthy bonds with caring people such as parents, particularly mothers and significant others, are essential dimensions in human development. Failure to generate strong and affirmative attachments threatens the development of a positive sense of an integrated self and of self-esteem.

Narcissism

According to Melvin R. Lansky, suicide is a real risk and, at the same time, "the suicidal patient becomes flooded with shame. Shame is the emotion that signals either the loss of meaningful bonding or the awareness of the impossibility of bonding in a meaningful generative way rather than an infantile one. Shame in this sense is both the premonitory danger signal and the catastrophic end-stage of narcissistic wounding."[58] The shame that results from the exposure of *narcissistic wounding* is what may trigger suicide and suicidal behaviors. Melvin Lansky is one of those who best emphasize the relationship among narcissism, shame and suicide:

> Suicidal crises, then, reflect a narcissistic breakdown, a collapse and exposure. It is important to realise that, clinically, we are usually dealing with bypassed shame. Bonds perpetuated on a basically shameful level in which a patient with an acute sense of shame, derived from either illness or early family upbringing, is threatened with exposure and loss of meaningful, albeit infantile bonds that help mask the shame. Bypassed shame has been exhaustively studied by Lewis (1971, 1987). Such unacknowledged shame has a great deal to do with generating hostile dependency and envy. . . . Theoretical discussions of hostility and envy usually overlook the significance of shame in the clinical picture.[59]

In his 1996 article "Shame and Suicide in Sophocles' *Ajax*," Lansky continues to analyze the link between narcissism and shame as a factor leading to suicide. According to him, and following the development of psychoanalytic theories on narcissism, particularly that of S. Freud and K. Abraham, the study of shame increased "With exploration of narcissistic phenomena."[60] Lansky points out that "The ego ideal, that is, the standard in the face of which one might fail or be rejected, is the locus of shame."[61] Hence,

> Narcissistic pathology implies pathology of the ego ideal, of aspirations that are excessively harsh or unattainable rather than prohibitions. . . . Narcissistic pathology, by tolerating no discrepancy between the real and the ideal self, includes (and perhaps derives from) a pathological intolerance of shame. Accompanying this ego ideal pathology is the pathological need for a feeling of self-sufficiency, paradoxically accompanied by a need for others to affirm one's idealized views of oneself. Dependent on others for affirmation and accolades, such people are unable to tolerate the shame of acknowledging their true feelings of dependency on others and thus make pathological attempts to rid themselves of those feelings.[62]

Narcissistic people can become arrogant and frequently have the tendency to put others down, to make them feel ashamed and insignificant in order to keep themselves feeling superior. For Lansky, "very little has been published in the psychoanalytic literature on the sequences of narcissistic injury giving rise to shame and rageful attempts to restore a balance, often by attacking parties not at all involved in the original shaming and often at the cost of continued or enhanced rejection and more shame."[63] Similarly, Barry W. Shreve and Mark A. Kunkel underline how arrogance, one of the components of narcissism, can in fact be an unowned or bypassed manifestation of a shame-prone personality:

> An extreme example of an attempt to escape from the pain of shame is the suicidal act.
> Shame-motivated suicide, attempted suicide, and the contemplation of suicide as a method
> of escaping a profound sense of shame increasingly are being reported . . . as counselors
> and other mental health professionals look beyond the traditional loss-depression-anger
> models of suicidal behavior.[64]

Narcissism becomes, like substance abuse, a maladaptive way of dealing with chronic shame. Suicide is often its final and more extreme act.

In 1992 several publications appeared that dealt with the relationship among shame, narcissism and suicide. In an exploratory correlational study regarding narcissism, shame, masochism, and object relations, Stephen Hibbard emphasized how "there seems to be a consensus among theoreticians that the connection between shame and narcissism is through failure of the idealizing aspects of narcissism in faulty attempts at self-esteem regulation."[65] For his part, Nathanson, defining the self in psychoanalytic language, refers to the Freudian theory in which narcissism is almost the normal state of the infant, "until self and object are split apart by the forces of libido."[66] In Freudian theory, "Shame is viewed as the failure to renounce sexual exhibitionism–all shame is either vaguely or specifically sexual."[67] Presenting other theories regarding the development of the self from a psychoanalytic perspective, Nathanson points out:

> Acceptance of the Kohutian scheme of "narcissistic development" limits one's understanding
> of shame to those situations in which there has been a "narcissistic injury" or in which
> the sense of self has been damaged. Andrew Morrison, the self psychologist best known
> for his writings about shame, commented to me that "shame is an affective response to a
> perception of the self as flawed, and thus inevitably involves narcissism."[68]

According to Nathanson, narcissism is a way of withdrawing from the painful experience of shame, that is, "narcissism is the system through which personal attributes are exaggerated in order to avoid shame."[69] Nathanson does not completely accept Freudian theory regarding the fact that narcissism is a normal step in infant development. For Nathanson, infants are not completely concerned with self-regard. Rather, they communicate with their mother "through the language of innate affect."[70] He continues, "If we recognize that the normal infant is never narcissistic, it becomes clear that adult narcissism is only and always a protection against shame. Narcissism is the name we give to the broad array of scripts through which people prevent themselves from 'knowing' about anything that might increase an already unbearable amount of shame."[71] When withdrawal is not possible, when one feels that one's perceived deficient self is disclosed, suicide may become the final act of the wounded self.

Richard Gramzow and June Price Tangney, working with a sample of 215 undergraduate students in order to establish proneness to shame and narcissistic personality, also emphasize the relationship between shame and pathological narcissism.[72] The same position is taken by Michael Lewis. For him, "Shame bears on narcissism; indeed, the narcissistic personality is the personality of the shamed."[73] Narcissism is a manifestation of shame, either in a conscious or unacknowledged way: "Narcissism is the ultimate attempt to avoid shame."[74] For Lewis, there are two possible descriptions or conceptions of narcissism: one as a manifestation of people's actions, in which a person is performing, that is, looking for excellence, but without becoming dysfunctional–without performing and trying to excel at any cost–and another description which considers narcissism as a pathological disorder. He believes that the term "narcissism" should be used exclusively for dealing with the description of the pathological dimension of narcissism. In this sense, as also stated by Nathanson, Michael Lewis thinks that "narcissists are readily shame-prone and, because of this tendency, act to avoid experiencing shame. They try to avoid shame either by utilizing a set of ideations designed to avoid shame, or, when this process does not work, by engaging in emotional behavior that masks their underlying shame."[75]Again, suicide appears to be the final act by which a narcissistic person tries to avoid shame.[76]

Pathological narcissism, with its link to violence and shame, has also been discussed by Stewert L. Hockenberry. Narcissism, as a consequence of chronic shame, may bring one to behave in a violent way. According to him,

> the narcissistic personality has been described as suffering from a poorly developed self-concept and chronically low self-esteem, in which a complex range of compensatory defenses are mobilized in order to avoid further experiences of self-fragmentation, shame, and depression. . . . Included among these defenses are a grandiose sense of self-importance, pseudoautonomy (defensive self-sufficiency), a compulsive need to be prized and admired by others, and a need to control others as objects or extensions of oneself. These individuals characteristically approach relationships with a sense of entitlement, a lack of empathy, and a tendency to react with rage when shamed or criticized. In fact, shame

and rage have both been identified as principal affects experienced within narcissistic pathology.[77]

For Hockenberry, pathological narcissism is the result of having been exposed to excessive shame. Here, too, we can deduce that suicide is the final act by which a narcissistic personality protects itself against pathological shame.

In her study regarding suicide and internalized relationships from the perspective of psychotherapists working with suicidal patients, in which she surveyed one hundred psychotherapists, Barbara M. Richards also stresses that

> The data produced in the current study appear to suggest that the experience of the suicidal person is such that a present experience of loss reactivates past rejections and feelings of emptiness. When these patients experience loss, it is likely that they feel a narcissistic insult. It is not the size of the insult that matters; rather it is the meaning given to the event in the person's inner world that is important.[78]

Finally, Apter et al. highlight the important role that perfectionism and narcissism have on suicidal behavior. Referring to the sets of personality traits regarding suicidal tendencies, these authors state: "The first [set] includes narcissism, perfectionism, and the inability to tolerate failure and imperfection, combined with a schizoid personality structure that does not allow the individual to ask for help and denies him the comfort of intimacy."[79] Thus, perfectionism and narcissism conceal the destructive feelings of shame that are characteristic of the shame-prone personality. The suicidal act is viewed as the only exit from these painful experiences.

Conclusion

In this chapter I have presented some of the most important approaches to understanding shame as a factor in suicide or suicidal behavior: alienation from oneself and others, the chain reaction of hopelessness→depression→substance abuse→suicide and, finally, perfectionism and narcissism, being unowned or bypassed manifestations of shame.

These approaches have a few points in common. First, they underline the fact that the lack of social support has an influence on alienation from oneself and others and on hopelessness regarding the future, with its effects in depression and alcoholism. However, this lack of social support is often the consequence of a cognitive distortion of reality rather than being an established fact. A person believes that isolation, or feeling hopeless, is the result of a conscious attitude on the part of others, or of a situation without exit. But this can be simply the result of the person's own perception, which is often a distorted view of reality.

This cognitive distortion of reality, which is common in shame-prone personalities and carries with it the risk of leading to suicidal behavior, is something that needs to be assessed and treated carefully in order to avoid its potentially lethal consequences. We must provide tools that will help people, particularly adolescents and the elderly, who are the two populations at greatest risk for suicide, to develop problem-solving skills and to have a more objective cognitive perception of reality.

A second point that these approaches highlight is the lack of self-disclosure. The inability to disclose oneself to others easily impairs one's capacity to have stronger social supports and to receive the required help needed in order to overcome isolation and hopelessness. Often one does not know the needs of the other person. The inability to disclose one's intimate feelings and needs, the covering of the real self, are usually present in perfectionism and narcissism. So, one has to assess and to address in psychotherapy and, in a larger way, within the family and the educational environment, the importance of disclosing one's innermost feelings and needs.

The third point that these approaches emphasize is, as indicated in the previous chapter, that the recognition and integration of the painful experiences which trigger shame, and the importance of sharing them with significant others, are essential elements in overcoming their unhealthy influence in people's lives. To learn how to disclose or reveal oneself to others is, then, a key element in triumphing against factors which, in other circumstances, could lead to suicide as a final and despairing act of liberation from chronic shame.

Anyone who is an adult child of an alcoholic knows very well what alienation from oneself and others means and how difficult it is for a child to share with others one's innermost feelings such as fear and shame. The result can be hopelessness, depression, suicidal thoughts and having to become an adult very quickly. Besides, perfectionism and excessive concern for oneself, or narcissism resulting from not having strong emotional bonds during infancy and early childhood, have been factors which one needs to combat in order to overcome dysfunctional ways of being and unhealthy interactions acquired during the early stages of personality development. As already mentioned, sharing innermost feelings with others, particularly with significant ones, is the road to healing shame and overcoming its maladaptive consequences.

The first chapter presented the relationship between chronic shame and suicide. This second chapter surveyed current pictures of shame as a factor in suicide. Now it will be important to spell out a theoretical framework that will enable us to understand more easily the role chronic shame plays in respect to suicide. Establishing such a theoretical framework will be the purpose of the next chapter.

Notes

[1] Kalafat & Lester, 2000.

[2] Bradshaw, 1988; Conner et al., 2001.

[3] Bradshaw, 1988, p. 73.

[4] Breed, 1972, p. 8.

[5] Baumeister, 1990, p. 91.

[6] Baumeister, 1990, p. 95.

[7] Mauk & Weber, 1991, p. 113.

[8] Mauk & Weber, 1991, p. 114.

[9] Lansky, 1991, p. 232. Italics in the original text.

[10] Lansky, 1991, p. 232.

[11] Marttunen et al., 1993, p. 1182.

[12] Heikkinen, Aro, & Lönnqvist, 1993, p. 345.

[13] Jordan, 2001.

[14] Mokros, 1995, p. 1096.

[15] Klinger, 1999, p. 115.

[16] Beautrais, 2000, p. 424.

[17] Apter, Horesh, Gothelf, Graffi, & Lepkifker, 2001, p. 73.

[18] Beck, 1967, p. 264.

[19] Beck, 1967, p. 277.

[20] Beck, Kovacs, & Weissman, 1975, p. 1147.

[21] Beck et al., 1975, p. 1147.

[22] Beck et al., 1975, p. 1149.

[23] Williams & Pollock, 1993.

[24] Harry & Lennings, 1993, pp. 267–268.

[25] Rosenhan & Seligman, 1995, pp. 409–410.

[26] Clayton, 1993, p. 827.

[27] Clayton, 1993, p. 828.

[28] Stoelb & Chiriboga, 1998, p. 362.

[29] Kaplan et al., 1999, p. 985.

[30] Gust-Brey & Cross, 1999.

[31] Klinger, 1999, p. 116.

[32] Gutierrez, Osman, Kopper, Barrios, & Bagge, 2000, p. 403.

[33] Gutierrez et al., 2000, p. 410.

[34] Fritsch, Donaldson, Spirito, & Plummer, 2000, p. 221.

[35] Westefeld et al., 2000, p. 454.

[36] Apter et al., 2001.

[37] Goldston et al., 2001.

[38] Furr, McConnel, Westefeld, & Jenkins, 2001, p. 97.

[39] Van Ness & Larson, 2002, p. 393.

[40] Roff, 2001.

[41] Holden & Kroner, 2003, p. 36.

[42] Baumeister, 1990, p. 97.

[43] Hufford, 2001, p. 802.

[44] Hufford, 2001, p. 807.

[45] Roy, 1993, p. 133.

[46] Roy, 1993, p. 133.

[47] Roy, 1993, p. 134.

[48] Wasserman, 1993, p. 267.

[49] Roy, 2001, p. 120.

[50] Roy, 2001, p. 121.

[51] Bensley, Van Eenwyk, Spieker, & Schoder, 1999; Bifulco, Moran, Baines, Bunn, & Standord, 2002; Gould, Fisher, Parides, Flory, & Shaffer, 1996; Stanard, 2000; Vajda & Steinbeck, 2000.

[52] Lombardi, Florentino, & Lombardi, 1998, p. 61.

[53] Lombardi et al., 1998, p. 69.

[54] Pattison, 2000.

[55] Gust-Brey & Cross, 1999, p. 31.

[56] Rosenhan & Seligman, 1995, p. 587.

[57] Rosenhan & Seligman, 1995, p. 587.

[58] Lansky, 1991, p. 230.

[59] Lansky, 1991, pp. 233–234.

[60] Lansky, 1996, p. 768.

[61] Lansky, 1996, p. 769.

[62] Lansky, 1996, p. 769.

[63] Lansky, 1996, pp. 770–771.

[64] Shreve & Kunkel, 1991, p. 307.

[65] Hibbard, 1992, p. 504.

[66] Nathanson, 1992, p. 192.

[67] Nathanson, 1992, p. 195.

[68] Nathanson, 1992, p. 195.

[69] Nathanson, 1992, p. 348.

[70] Nathanson, 1992, p. 348.

[71] Nathanson, 1992, p. 348.

[72] Gramzow & Tangney, 1992.

[73] Lewis, 1992, p. 2.

[74] Lewis, 1992, p. 2.

[75] Lewis, 1992, p. 165.

[76] Fasullo & Guarneri, 1993; Pattison, 2000.

[77] Hockenberry, 1995, pp. 302–303.

[78] Richards, 1999, pp. 91–92.

[79] Apter et al., 2001, p. 70.

Chapter III

Lazarus and Folkman on Stress, Shame, Suicide

In the previous two chapters, I presented the multiple dimensions of shame and how, in fact, suicide is the last step, certainly the most lethal one, in coping with excessive shame. In addition, I have shown that there are many ways in which the relationship between shame and suicide appears to be evident. In this chapter, I wish to present the theory of coping with stress that Lazarus and Folkman propose[1] as a conceptual framework that can be applied to the interaction between shame and suicide.

Thus, I begin by introducing Lazarus and Folkman's theory of coping with stress and focus on its development and effectiveness. To deal with shame, suicide and the bereavement process is one of the most stressful experiences of life. Furthermore, this theory of coping with stress has become a point of reference for further research.

In the second part of this chapter, following Lazarus and Folkman's theory, I wish to show how shame is a personal and environmental constraint that makes it difficult to cope with suicide in a healthy way. After presenting what Lazarus and Folkman understand by personal and environmental constraints against coping with stress, I shall try to justify the application of their understanding to my own research.

Finally, in a third section of this chapter, I shall explain the two roles of religion in its link with shame and suicide. Religion can help us to cope with suicide in a constructive way. At the same time, it can become an inhibitor: it can keep us from dealing with this stressful event in a healthy manner.

Coping with Stress

Richard S. Lazarus is one of the most important scholars and a leading psychologist specializing in the area of coping with stress. In 1966 he published *Psychological Stress and the Coping Process*, a pioneering work in the field. As he himself notes in the preface of the book: "At the psychological level of analysis, there is not a single book that draws upon the many varieties of research that make up the empirical side of the field. I wrote this book to fill this gap. It is a general attempt at systematization of concepts, language, and observation."[2] This task of systematization resulted in presenting stress "as an organizing concept." Lazarus and Folkman write in relation to this: "In 1966 Lazarus suggested that stress be treated as an organizing concept for understanding a wide range of phenomena of great importance in human and animal adaptation. Stress, then, is not a variable but a rubric consisting of many variables and processes. We still believe that this is the most useful approach to take."[3]

There are three major concepts in the theory that Lazarus developed in 1966 that have been broadened by Lazarus and Folkman: *stress, appraisal,* and *coping.* First, "*Psychological stress is a particular relationship between the person and the environment that is appraised by the person as taxing or exceeding his or her resources and endangering his or her well-being.*"[4] From being considered as the result of external influences upon the person, stress is now viewed in a more integral perspective where the person plays an important role.

Second, in this relationship between the person and the environment there is an essential moment that consists of an evaluation of the situation, a cognitive appraisal before any coping occurs:

> Cognitive appraisal is an evaluative process that determines why and to what extent a particular transaction or series of transactions between the person and the environment is stressful. Coping is the process through which the individual manages the demands of the person-environment relationship that are appraised as stressful and the emotions they generate.[5]

Lazarus points out what he and Folkman later developed regarding the two dimensions of the evaluative process or appraisal: *primary* and *secondary* appraisal. At the beginning, the person must evaluate the degree of danger being encountered. In this sense, "Stressful appraisals can take three forms: harm/loss, threat, and challenge."[6] Once the person assesses the degree of danger found in the environment, the next step consists in seeing what strategies are the most appropriate for coping with the situation and the results that will derive from it:

> Secondary appraisal is a judgment concerning what might and can be done. It includes an evaluation about whether a given coping option will accomplish what it is supposed to, that one can apply a particular strategy or set of strategies effectively, and an evaluation of the consequences of using a particular strategy in the context of other internal and/or external demands and constraints.[7]

Nevertheless, from the publication of Lazarus in 1966 and of Lazarus and Folkman in 1984, it appears that there is a clear relationship between primary and secondary appraisal. Even if each of them is concerned with specific dimensions of the problem, "primary appraisals can influence secondary appraisals, and vice versa."[8] Both appraisals are necessary in order to evaluate "the degree of stress and the strength and quality (or content) of the emotional reaction."[9] Furthermore, Lazarus and Folkman also introduce another dimension in the appraisal process called *reappraisal:* "Reappraisal refers to a changed appraisal on the basis of new information from the environment."[10]

According to both publications, one has to consider both the personal and the situational factors influencing appraisal. That is, everything related to the person, for example, beliefs, commitments, and emotions, acts upon the cognitive process implicated in appraisal. Finally, "one must remember that situation and person factors are always interdependent, and their significance for stress and coping derives from the operation of cognitive processes that give weight to one in the context of the other."[11] Pure objectivity or subjectivity is quite impossible. As a proverb says: "Each one sees the world with the color of her or his sunglasses."

Third, the originality of Lazarus's and Folkman's theory of psychological stress lies not only in the conception of stress as an interaction and appraisal as a process, but also in the interpretation of coping as a process. If in 1966 Lazarus uses the term *coping* for "referring to strategies for dealing with threat,"[12] in 1984 Lazarus and Folkman distinguish two approaches to coping, one found in the animal experimentation model, in which "coping is frequently defined as acts that control aversive environment conditions, thereby lowering psychophysiological disturbance,"[13] and the other

> In the psychoanalytic ego psychology model, [where] coping is defined as realistic and flexible thoughts and acts that solve problems and thereby reduce stress. The main difference between the treatment of coping in this model compared to the animal model is the focus on ways of perceiving and thinking about the person's relationship with the environment. Although behavior is not ignored, it is treated as less important than cognition.[14]

If, in the animal model, coping consists in acts and reactions for controlling aversive situations, and one can image these reactions as being irrational, in the psychoanalytic model the process of cognitive appraisal is essential.

In the next section of this chapter I shall continue to develop Lazarus and Folkman's theory of coping with stress, along with a consideration of the different constraints against coping. Nonetheless, I would like to emphasize here that in his book of 1999, *Stress and Emotion: A New Synthesis*, Richard S. Lazarus elaborates the essence of what he and Folkman wrote in 1984. The originality of the more recent publication lies, according to Lazarus, in the following:

The most important topical additions to this version are, first, an attempt to integrate the fields of stress and emotion, which have always belonged together but have traditionally been treated separately. Second, I have proposed that we move beyond a systems approach, which is probably not practical in today's research world, and turn to a narrative theoretical and research approach that I now believe is the most promising way to examine the dynamics of stress and emotion from both a variable-centered and person-centered perspective.[15]

In 1984, when Lazarus wrote the book with Folkman, and still less in 1966, when he wrote *Psychological Stress and the Coping Process*, interest in stress and emotion was not as generalized as when he published his book in 1999. In that book he emphasized the unity among stress, emotion and coping. According to him, "The three concepts, stress, emotion, and coping, belong together and form a conceptual unit, with emotion being the superordinate concept because it includes stress and coping."[16] Lazarus considers shame as an existential emotion which consists in a failure to live according to an ego-ideal. Moreover, "Shame-ridden persons may be more prone to suicide, which [as indicated in the first chapter] is a common mode of coping in Japan when one's actions are condemned."[17] Furthermore, Lazarus develops his working assumptions on stress, which are "(a) the psychology of interaction, transaction, and relational meanings; (b) process and structure; (c) analysis and synthesis; and (d) systems theory."[18] These epistemological and metatheoretical issues and principles can be considered "as a series of contrasts, for example, *interaction versus transaction and relational meaning, structure versus process, analysis versus synthesis,* and *linear analysis versus systems theory.*"[19]

The theories of Lazarus, and particularly those of Lazarus and Folkman, regarding stress, appraisal and coping have been very well received, and have proven to be effective. In 1992, Meinrad Perrer and Michael Reicherts published *Stress, Coping, and Health: A Situation-Behavior Approach: Theory, Methods, Applications,* with a foreword by Richard S. Lazarus in which he indicates how Perrez and Reicherts

carry stress and coping theory and research beyond the point where Folkman and I were able to take it. . . . It is, therefore, a pleasure to have the opportunity to write a foreword to this book because the research and ideas reported are, in my opinion, serious and successful efforts to advance our understanding of the stress and coping process beyond previous work.[20]

Perrez and Reicherts recognize that the concepts introduced by Lazarus and Folkman "are part of today's basic vocabulary."[21] In addition, they, themselves bring new approaches to the assessment of stress and coping, applying them in clinical and health psychology.

Utilizing the theory of Lazarus and Folkman, Linda Kurtz and Jeffrey L. Derevensky, analyze the problem of stress and coping in adolescents within the context of the influence of family configuration and environment on suicide-related events. They examine the way in which personal characteristics such as perceptions and beliefs have an important influence in cognitive appraisal and in coping with stressful life experiences.[22]

Finally, Carolyn M. Aldwin presents an integrative perspective on stress, coping and development, which supports Lazarus. Her book contains a foreword by Lazarus in which he states that "Coping research and theory now seem to be on a fast track, with many studies being done and debates taking place about how we should approach the topic, both in measurement and theory. To someone who was a pioneer in this territory, the widespread interest is gratifying."[23] According to Lazarus, the originality of Aldwin's book consists in considering coping in an integrative way. This appears to be clearly indicated in the book's preface, where Aldwin speaks about its purpose: "Thus, I thought it was time for an integrative approach, one which attempted to dispassionately examine the pros and cons of all the myriad approaches in the area, identifying their strengths and weaknesses and specifying the circumstances under which the various approaches were more or less appropriate."[24] Aldwin's main contribution has been to introduce the concept of the "transactionist paradigm" in order to understand an integrative perspective:

> I believe we are currently undergoing another paradigm shift–from causal reductionism to transactionism. Simply put, in causal reductionism the occurrence of an event is reduced to its underlying cause, whereas in transactionism the occurrence of an event is understood to arise from the mutual influence of a number of factors. This paradigm shift has profound implications, not only for research and clinical practice, but also for the very fabric of society and how we conduct our everyday lives.[25]

Culture and the Person

As indicated by Lazarus and Folkman, an interaction between the person and the environment needs to be taken into consideration in order to understand psychological stress better. What Aldwin highlights regarding the influence of culture in the process of stress and coping is extremely important:

> Culture can affect the stress and coping process in four ways. First, the cultural context shapes the types of stressors that an individual is likely to experience. Second, culture may also affect the appraisal of the stressfulness of a given event. Third, cultures affect the choice of coping strategies that an individual utilizes in any given situation. Finally, the culture provides different institutional mechanisms by which an individual can cope with stress.[26]

Given this point, a number of observations are in order. (1) Shame can be used as a socio-cultural and/or religious stressor which impairs the capacity of people to deal with painful experiences such as suicide, and/or as a way of controlling people's behavior. (2) How one evaluates a situation depends on the values received from one's culture. If in a given culture one normally considers an event shameful, this can distort the evaluation one makes about the event, namely, it can be viewed as something wrong. (3) Suicide can be considered as a normal way of coping with chronic shame in some cultures, such as the Japanese, but not in others. (4) The number of resources available for dealing with bereavement can vary from one culture to another. The manner of sharing innermost feelings, which can help the grieving process, is different from one culture to another. In reality, Aldwin's position about the importance of culture in the process of stress and coping is close to what Lazarus and Folkman said in 1984 and Lazarus developed in 1999 regarding the personal and environmental constraints that, like culture, can act against the right use of appropriate resources for coping.

Shame as Personal: Problems in Coping with Suicide

We have just seen how coping with stress is a process through which the person deals with the requests of the interaction between person and environment. It consists in a series of strategies for confronting the challenges that the person experiences. In order to accomplish this task, the person has to perform a cognitive appraisal, that is, to carry out "realistic and flexible thoughts and acts that solve problems and thereby reduce stress."[27]

In coping with stress, as in the evaluative process or cognitive appraisal, not only external influences but also personality factors, such as general beliefs about reality, affect the process of coping. Lazarus and Folkman define these personal and environmental factors affecting coping as *constraints* against utilizing coping resources. They emphasize:

> The novelty and complexity of many stressful encounters create demands that often exceed the person's resources. For many occasions, however, resources are in fact adequate, but the person does not use them to their fullest because to do so might create additional conflict and distress. The factors that restrict the ways an individual deals with the environment may be called constraints, some of which arise from personal agendas, others of which are environmental.[28]

Personal agendas is another way of naming personal constraints. These are, among others, culturally derived values and beliefs that condition the ways in which a person is expected to behave in particular circumstances. These personal agendas are very important in the coping process. In the last chapter it was shown how cognitive distortions of reality are at the heart of hopelessness regarding the future, with its consequences for depression, substance abuse and suicide. Shame can also be considered as a personal agenda that impairs the possibility of having a more objective comprehension of reality.

Environmental constraints, exist outside of the person, for example, the number of resources available, or the use of these resources, or the way in which public institutions are or are not helping in the coping process. Here, too, shame can be considered an environmental constraint. It can be rooted in the culture or the way in which society and religion view a particular event. In any case, both dimensions of constraint, *personal* and *environmental*, are essential for understanding the coping process. We should note that in this research I am using "environmental" to refer to everything that comes from outside of the individual, whether familial, socio-cultural, or religious influences which can serve as inhibitors to and in the coping process.

Finally, as I have pointed out in the Introduction to this study, constraints can be considered "inhibitors of the effective use of coping resources,"[29] or, according to Lazarus and Folkman, "constraints can also be facilitative"[30] of the coping process.

The Lazarus and Folkman theory of stress, appraisal and coping helps us better understand both what has been presented in the previous two chapters and what will follow in the next one. There is no doubt that chronic shame is, on two counts, an inhibitor of coping in a healthy way with suicide-related events. First, suicide can be a result of excessive shame. Suicide is the way in which some shame-prone personalities cope with this painful experience. Second, undue shame can also be a constraint, making it more difficult to cope with suicide or attempted suicide and to participate in the bereavement process. A person who did not succeed in committing suicide can find it very difficult to cope with his or her present situation because the reaction of others can generate or aggravate shame. Eventually, this person may risk attempting suicide again, this time with higher probabilities of succeeding. Furthermore, the bereavement process related to a suicide can be impaired by feelings of shame because of the socio-cultural and religious stigma attached to suicide.

In both cases, whether suicide is a result of chronic shame or whether excessive shame is a way of giving a bias or particular direction to the bereavement process, toxic shame acts as an inhibitor, making it difficult for a person to cope in a positive manner with suicide-related events. In fact, pathological shame is an impediment to living a fulfilled life in all senses of the word. This applies to both the *personal* and *environmental* dimensions of constraint. Chronic shame can be a characteristic of a person but can also be present in the environment, family, society, culture and religion, and can impede the person's growing up in a mature way.

In summary, our recognition of *stress* as an interaction, *appraisal* (cognitive evaluation) and *coping* as a process, and *emotion* as a superordinate concept, will enable us to understand better the dynamic between shame and suicide. As an emotion, chronic shame plays a very important and distorting role in the cognitive evaluation of the interaction between the person and the environment that can then lead the person to commit suicide or to behave in a suicidal way.

I shall now present two different roles religion can play in the process of coping with suicide-related events. It can facilitate the process, helping the person to manage this painful experience in a positive way, or it can become a factor inhibiting the person from coping with suicide, impeding his or her ability to deal with it in a healthy manner.

Religion, Shame, Suicide

Lillian M. Range et al., in their research about multicultural perspectives on suicide, underline the twofold role of religion in relation to suicide. "The Catholic doctrine," they say, "teaches that it is a sin to take a life under any circumstance, so that religious beliefs may also serve as a buffer against suicide in Hispanic culture. Empirical research supports this conclusion: church attendance and being a born-again Christian are predictors of an absence of suicidal ideas."[31] Nevertheless, they add, "in all of these religions/philosophical views [Asian Americans], committing suicide may be preferable to remaining alive if the suicide protects the family from shame, exposure, or embarrassment."[32] Before continuing, it will be important to refer very briefly to the position of the Bible and the Rabbinic literature on suicide.

According to James T. Clemons, the "Hebrew Scriptures provide six accounts of direct suicide and the New Testament provides one."[33] After an attentive analysis of these accounts, Clemons concludes "that each [account] was told without a clear intention of condemning the act. Although in some cases the person who chose suicide was condemned by the historian, that negative judgment was always based on how the person had lived, not how they chose to die."[34] In any case, during the following centuries, "a wide variety of biblical texts have been used both to condemn and to condone the acts of suicide and attempted suicide."[35] In taking into account what the Bible expresses regarding suicide, one needs to be conscious of the fact that the Bible is not "a manual of dogmatic and moral theology that provides concrete, universally applicable answers to each and every moral question that life poses."[36] How what the Bible says regarding suicide has been interpreted through the varying socio-cultural and religious contexts of different periods of history is, then, another question.

Sidney Goldstein's study on suicide in the Rabbinic literature arrives at the same conclusion as Clemons. For Goldstein, "The Bible does not have an explicit prohibition against suicide."[37] This, he emphasizes, is also the position of the Torah and of the New Testament: "Although suicide is viewed with the utmost severity by many authorities and often spoken of in the most condemnatory terms, there is no explicit statement in the Torah prohibiting it."[38]

The attitude regarding suicide changed during the Christian era: "St. Augustine [354–430 A.D.] was the first to denounce suicide as a crime under all circumstances. This was to serve as the basic position of the Catholic Church even to the present day."[39] Nonetheless, as will be indicated below, Goldstein's second statement concerning the position of the Roman Catholic Church today is no longer accurate.

In fact, in canon 1240.1 of the *Codex Iuris Canonici [Codex of Canon Law]* of 1917, the Roman Catholic Church forbade the Christian burial of those who committed suicide. As Range et al. highlight, suicide was considered a grave sin. While still regarding suicide as something that "contradicts the natural inclination of the human being to preserve and perpetuate his life,"[40] the Roman Catholic Church makes an important, if difficult, distinction between an intentional-rational suicide and suicide as the result of "grave psychological disturbances, anguish or grave fear of hardship, suffering or torture [that] can diminish the responsibility of the one committing suicide."[41] The Roman Catholic Church no longer speaks of the eternal damnation of those who commit suicide. This change took place already "in the Roman Catholic canon law in 1983."[42] Therefore, "We should not despair of the eternal salvation of persons who have taken their own lives. By ways known to him alone, God can provide the opportunity for salutary repentance. The Church prays for persons who have taken their own lives."[43] This also means that there is no longer an interdiction of Christian burial for those who commit suicide.

The doctrinal and pastoral norms that the Roman Catholic Church had regarding suicide until not so long ago were not exclusive to the Church. The same norms were held by other Christian churches, or other religions and ethnic denominations. Thus, for example, Norman Doe, in his book *Canon Law in the Anglican Communion: A Worldwide Perspective*, in speaking about the disposal of human remains, emphasizes the great diversity among Anglican churches regarding death, funerals and the disposal of human remains. According to him, this is something that is treated more frequently by liturgical norms or quasi-legislation. Nonetheless, regarding the right of being buried in the parish churchyard and those that could be excluded, such as those who commit suicide, Doe says:

> In England today, any person who dies in a parish has a legal right to be buried in the parish churchyard in accordance with the funeral rites of the Church of England. A similar approach is adopted in Wales and Ireland. However, for most churches the principle is implicit within provisions dealing with denial of funeral rites to those who have died unbaptized, to suicides and to excommunicate persons. In some churches these classes are excluded from enjoyment of funeral rites and a special episcopally approved form of service must be used, usually where there is no evidence of repentance before death. The laws of a few churches confer on the minister a discretion to refuse to use the church's funeral rites in these cases.[44]

To my knowledge, there are presently no particular liturgical norms for dealing with the funeral or burial of people who committed suicide. Perhaps this silence is the best way of coping with the question.

Exline, Yali, and Sanderson, in analyzing the role of religious strain in depression and suicide-related events, also point out the twofold role of religion in relation to suicide. According to them,

> Religious life can be a locus of both comfort and strain. Although participants in both of these studies saw more good than bad when reflecting on their religious lives, the presence of religious strain emerged as a major indicator of psychological distress. Religious strain was associated with greater depression and suicidality, and these associations existed regardless of religiosity levels or the degree of comfort found in religion. These findings suggest that regardless of whether religion is a positive force in a person's life, the presence of religious strain may still warrant clinical attention.[45]

The position of Exline et al. regarding the role of religion in its relationship with suicide-related events is shared by Pattison, who speaks about the influence of religion, Christianity in particular, on shame. For him, "like other social institutions, [Christianity] engenders and promotes shame, often to enhance order and control,"[46] even if Christianity "can also diminish and alleviate shame, enhancing worth, efficacy and esteem."[47] Therefore, as seen above, it was necessary to make a distinction between Christianity and the Bible. Whereas Christianity has varied in its dealing with the question of suicide, the Bible reveals a God who constantly comes to meet people, even those considered "sinners," to offer them the divine love and the possibility of a new beginning in life. Moreover, the divine love liberates from shame and guilt.

Finally, in presenting international perspectives on suicide, assisted suicide and euthanasia, Leenaars and Connolly summarize very well what has been said so far concerning religion and suicide:

The Old Testament of the Western world does not directly forbid suicide, but in Jewish law suicide is wrong. During the early Christian years, there was excessive martyrdom, ie. suicide, resulting in considerable concern on the part of the Church Fathers. St Augustine (354–430 AD) categorically rejected suicide. Suicide was considered a sin because it violated the Sixth Commandment, "Thou shalt not kill". By 693 AD, the Church of the Council of Toledo proclaimed that individuals who attempted suicide should be excommunicated. St Thomas Aquinas (1225–1274 AD) espoused suicide to be a grave mortal sin. The notion of suicide as sin took firm hold in the West for hundreds of years. Only during the Renaissance and the Reformation did a different view emerge.[48]

Nonetheless, what Leenaars and Connolly say is no longer the position of the majority of churches, whatever their doctrinal denominations. In the same vein, Sharri Roff's affirmation must be considered out of date: "certain religious (i.e., Catholics and Jews), as well as ethnic groups like the Chinese, do not sanction suicide. These groups often refuse burial rites to members that commit suicide and, therefore, incidents of such may be underreported."[49]

Medicine, psychiatry, psychology, anthropology and sociology have contributed to the development of a more complete understanding of the complexities of suicidal behavior. Nonetheless, this does not mean that in reality, as will be indicated in the third part of the next chapter, suicide no longer bears a social, cultural and religious stigma.

In summary, even if we recognize that religion can contribute to or facilitate the coping process, namely, by enhancing people's resistance in the face of adversity, nevertheless, there is no doubt that it can be a source of fear, guilt and shame. For example, a particular way of preaching about sin and evil, or of teaching morality, has contributed to developing a feeling of guilt and shame in some people's lives. If we take into consideration that suicide was viewed as a sin until quite recently in several religious denominations, there is no doubt that this was a constraint to survivors of suicide and to those who attempted suicide. This situation made it more difficult to cope in a positive way with the bereavement process and aftermath of a suicide.

Conclusion

In the last chapter, I highlighted the fact that cognitive distortions of reality can have lethal consequences because of their influence on hopelessness, depression, substance abuse, and suicidal behavior. Following Lazarus and Folkman's theory, we can now say that cognitive distortions of reality belong to the personal constraints or personal agendas that impair the capacity for developing a more objective perception of a situation. As a result, the situation can become so stressful that it can lead a person to commit suicide.

In this chapter, I tried to demonstrate how the theory of Lazarus and Folkman regarding stress, appraisal and coping can be used as a theoretical framework to work out a better understanding of the role of shame in relation to suicide. In fact, shame can be seen as a personal and environmental constraint making it difficult to cope with suicidal behavior in a healthy way. Shame can function as something that inhibits, reduces or impairs the resources that the person can use for dealing with suicide-related events.

Finally, following the two meanings that constraint has in Lazarus and Folkman, I pointed out how religion can act as an *inhibitor* or *facilitator* of the coping process. Religion can help people deal with suicide in a healthy way. At the same time, it can inhibit coping in a positive manner with suicide-related events. It can trigger suicide and suicidal behavior because the person may either feel extremely guilty and ashamed of himself or herself or even consider suicide a more or less accepted way of dealing with shameful events. How shame can be a constraint against coping in a healthy way with suicide will be discussed in the next chapter.

Notes

1   Lazarus & Folkman, 1984.
2   Lazarus, 1966, p. vii.
3   Lazarus & Folkman, 1984, pp. 11–12.
4   Lazarus & Folkman, 1984, p. 19. Italics in the original text.
5   Lazarus & Folkman, 1984, p. 19.
6   Lazarus & Folkman, 1984, p. 53.
7   Lazarus & Folkman, 1984, p. 53.
8   Lazarus, 1966, p. 161.
9   Lazarus & Folkman, 1984, p. 35.
10 Lazarus & Folkman, 1984, p. 38.
11 Lazarus & Folkman, 1984, p. 116.
12 Lazarus, 1966, p. 151.
13 Lazarus & Folkman, 1984, p. 118.
14 Lazarus & Folkman, 1984, p. 118.
15 Lazarus, 1999, pp. xiii–xiv.
16 Lazarus, 1999, p. 37.
17 Lazarus, 1999, p. 240.
18 Lazarus, 1999, p. 12.
19 Lazarus, 1999, p. 23. Italics in the original text.
20 Perrez & Reicherts, 1992, pp. 6–7.
21 Perrez & Reicherts, 1992, p. 17.
22 Kurtz & Derevensky, 1993.
23 Aldwin, 1994, p. v.
24 Aldwin, 1994, p. xiv.
25 Aldwin, 1994, p. 1.
26 Aldwin, 1994, p. 193.
27 Lazarus & Folkman, 1984, p. 118.
28 Lazarus & Folkman, 1984, p. 165.
29 Lazarus & Folkman, 1984, p. 167.
30 Lazarus & Folkman, 1984, p. 167.
31 Range et al., 1999, p. 418.
32 Range et al., 1999, p. 422.
33 Clemons, 1990, p. 15.
34 Clemons, 1990, pp. 27–28.
35 Clemons, 1990, p. 29.
36 Vogels, 2003, p. 147.
37 Goldstein, 1989, p. 3.
38 Goldstein, 1989, p. 51.
39 Goldstein, 1989, p. 68.

[40]   *Catechism of the Catholic Church [C.C.C.]*, 1993, no. 2281.

[41]   *C.C.C.*, 1993, no. 2282.

[42]   Clemons, 1990, p. 86.

[43]   *C.C.C.*, 1993, no. 2283.

[44]   Doe, 1998, pp. 298–299.

[45]   Exline, Yali, & Sanderson, 2000, p. 1490.

[46]   Pattison, 2000, p. 229.

[47]   Pattison, 2000, p. 229.

[48]   Leenaars & Connolly, 2001, p. 34.

[49]   Roff, 2001, p. 31.

Chapter IV

Shame and Suicide Survivors

In his presidential address at the annual meeting of the American Association of Suicidology, on April 26, 1990, in New Orleans, Louisiana, Robert I. Yufit underlined the most important themes dealing with suicide and what further research needs to be undertaken in the next ten years. First, he said, "we must vastly improve our existing clinical assessment techniques, or develop better ones."[1] Second, taking into consideration the particular risk of suicide among adolescents, he added:

> in the long run we must expand school programs to help educate our young people on how to cope better with stress and how to deal with loss, failure, shame, guilt, humiliation, and rejection. Such school education programs pose a long-range goal, to help both children and adults cope with stress more effectively, and by so doing minimize suicide as an option in problem solution. This objective of developing new and better instruments could take a decade to accomplish.[2]

Finally, at the end of his address, speaking about three reasons for justifying the importance of having better assessment procedures, he emphasized:

> A third very important reason is to decrease the suffering of survivors, who must deal with the effects of such loss or injury, for the remainder of their lives. The enormous psychological pain and change in subsequent lifestyle endured by survivors is immeasurable, and should be carefully studied with the aim of learning how to increase skills in coping with such loss.[3]

In fact, during the past decade, research carried out regarding the problematic of suicide responds to the major points Yufit raised in 1990. I am especially convinced that studies on suicide survivors are essential. As I have highlighted in the Introduction to this study, suicide affects not only the person who commits it, but also many other people. In fact, a survivor is "any person who has been affected by a loss through suicide. Survivors are family members, friends, lovers, colleagues, neighbors, schoolmates, therapists, even community."[4] These are individuals who are not indifferent in the face of such an extreme action.

However, in contrast to research done in the area of guilt feelings, little attention has been paid to the special relationship between shame and survivors of suicide, particularly when we consider that shame is an emotion engendering several other reactions. Thus, I find it necessary to make this link more explicit in this chapter. It is my belief, following the theory of Lazarus and Folkman on coping with stress presented in the previous chapter, that shame is also a personal and environmental constraint against coping appropriately with the bereavement process; that is, it negatively affects the capacity of survivors of suicide to follow through on that process.

Shame, as I indicate in the first part of this chapter, plays an important and negative role in the life of those who unsuccessfully attempt suicide. Frequently, the situation after the suicide attempt can become so painful and shameful that the person risks re-attempting suicide, this time with higher chances of succeeding.

Furthermore, shame affects the bereavement process in a particular way. As a result, the feelings and emotions experienced by survivors of suicide are, as will be emphasized in the second part of this chapter, more intense and longer lasting than feelings and emotions present in survivors of people who have died in other ways.

Finally, in the third part of this chapter, and in relation to the previous two parts, I analyze how social, cultural and religious stigma attached to suicide also impair the bereavement process. Even if, as I have indicated earlier, the attitudes of the majority of religious denominations have changed regarding suicide, the fact is that it continues to be considered a stigmatized and stigmatizing event and the stigma deeply affects survivors. In reality, the stigma attached to suicide can be seen as both a consequence and a source of shame. Here, shame can be regarded as an environmental constraint against coping with suicide in a positive manner.

Attempts and Successes in Suicide

In the first two chapters of this study, I discussed the specific relationship between shame and suicide. Suicide is the most extreme way of coping with chronic shame. Even though not all of those who attempt suicide succeed, another problem arises, namely, re-attempting suicide. Unfortunately, the person often makes another attempt at suicide within a relatively short period of time, and many times has a higher chance of succeeding.

Many factors are associated with repeated suicide attempts. One is "the realization of a suicide attempt, and the presence of a mental disorder."[5] As such, attempting suicide without succeeding is already a risk that can lead one to try again. In the introduction to their research, Tejedor et al. point out that with regard to suicide attempts and re-attempts:

> a series of suicidal risk factors have been confirmed repeatedly, the most noteworthy being
> mental disorders (depression and alcoholism are associated with almost 50% of all

suicides), previous suicide attempts, male gender, older age, the presence of physical illness and a poor social network. With regard to reattempts, in addition to these factors other variables have been described, namely female gender, young age, being unemployed, social discrimination, stressful life events and substance abuse.[6]

We must consider here the role of shame in the suicidal risk factors described above. It is important to realize that the particular function that shame plays on women, in the lives of adolescents, on unemployed people, in social discrimination, and in various stressful life events, can become a trigger for re-attempting suicide.

Furthermore, the attempt once made, together with substance abuse of any kind, psycho-affective disorders and sexual abuse, all factors intrinsically linked to shame, often leads to a re-attempt within 12 months after the earlier one, especially among adolescents. "Older patients and those suffering from schizophrenic disorders relapse over a longer period."[7] Consequently, in the prevention of re-attempted suicide, one needs to pay firsthand attention to those who are experiencing the previously listed risk factors.

Given the abundant quantity of research regarding survivors of suicide, and the risk of re-attempts, it is surprising to note the lack of empirical studies on the important relationship between unsuccessful suicide attempts and shame. We need to recognize this lack and to review our previous observations in this study about unowned or bypassed shame and suicide. Given the stigma attached to suicide, it would not be difficult to understand how those not succeeding in a suicide attempt must feel stigmatized and suffer so shameful and difficult an experience that they try again and, in many cases, succeed. For this reason, I consider it essential that future research and therapy pay more attention to the importance of shame for those who attempt suicide without succeeding, in order to prevent the danger of another attempt.

Suicide and Bereavement

As indicated above, during the past ten years much research has been done on suicide survivors. Generally speaking, all of this research highlights the particular reactions and feelings they experience in comparison with reactions and feelings manifested in survivors of other kinds of death. Suicide survivors share some common dimensions with others who grieve the death of a close one, particularly when the death occurred tragically or violently, due to accident, homicide, or unexpected natural causes. But my intention here is to emphasize suicide survivors' specific reactions and emotions, especially the negative role that shame plays in the bereavement process. For Rowe, "The shame and selective unawareness with which the law, society and families treat suicide are well documented in the literature on suicide."[8] Shame functions here as a personal and environmental constraint which impairs the bereavement process in various ways. The expressions of shame are well known: the taboo, stigma, secrecy, denial and silence regarding the circumstances of the death; the lack of opportunities or willingness to share feelings and emotions among survivors who consider themselves rejected by others; the presence of depression, self-blame or blaming each other in the family; feelings of social isolation, or changes of residence; and even the risk of suicide or attempting suicide. All of these feelings and emotions are commonly found among suicide survivors.

I shall follow here a chronological approach in presenting the most important dimensions of research done on suicide survivors in relationship to shame. Robert G. Dunn and Donna Morrish-Vidners summarize quite well the "atypical" bereavement process among suicide survivors:

> The shock and pain following this type of death engender grief of an unusual intensity. Given the nature of the suicidal act, and the situation of the bereaved, extensive blaming accompanies the grief process. Moreover, since suicide is still socially unacceptable, the bereaved lack the support systems normally available to those grieving other kinds of death. Consequently, the suicide survivor is placed in a kind of double jeopardy. On the one hand, the survivor suffers a traumatic loss; on the other hand, the taboo act generates feelings of disapproval and shame. The abnormality of suicide leads to a condition of normlessness, leaving the survivor without cultural guidelines and social support to guide the bereavement process. As a result, the survivor is forced into a privatized and individualistic mode of grieving, further aggravating the unique difficulties of adjustment following sudden and self-inflicted death. Finally, unlike most other kinds of death, suicide provokes an emotional and moral crisis which can produce dramatic inner changes, often leading to the personal transformation of the bereaved.[9]

These authors eloquently indicate that society still considers suicide unacceptable. When we consider that mourning, the social expression of bereavement, is largely conditioned by socio-cultural and religious norms,[10] we see that suicide survivors often experience social isolation, which further increases the taboo regarding suicide and associated feelings of shame. Nonetheless, the bereavement process also offers them the possibility of a greater transformation in their way of living, as will be emphasized below.

Survivors and Bereavement

Presenting the development of the Grief Experience Questionnaire, and the particularity of certain reactions among survivors of suicide, Terence W. Barret and

Thomas B. Scott are among the few who underline the specific character of shame as one of the predominant emotions of survivors that condition other behavior:

> Unlike other survivors, survivors of suicide are likely to experience a sense of shame and embarrassment about the nature of the death and report feelings of shame at having to tell others that a family member died by suicide. . . . The experience of shame may result in a frequent denial of the cause of the death and in an inability to talk openly and honestly about the death.[11]

These findings are often supported by research done on suicide survivors. However, perhaps one of the most important points characterizing the situation of suicide survivors, in contrast to that of survivors of other kinds of death, is that "grief over the death may be only the beginning of tremendous grief over many other issues that must be grieved for, for a complete and healthy healing and recovery."[12] In fact, suicide challenges all the dynamics and the interaction that would normally go on within families and among variously related persons. For this reason, it is not surprising that, frequently, the taboo regarding suicide is not only a way to avoid shame and social stigma, but also a way to elude confrontation within the family itself. Thus, as Gyulay indicates, "This 'secret' is often carried by many family members, who may never, or rarely, share it with each other. This secret burden may eventually, usually years after the death, be shared between family members. A young woman finally shared her concern with her mother 10 years after the death."[13] This silence acts as a poison for survivors, preventing them from having a more fulfilling life.

In addition, "Extended denial allows the survivor to run from the reality of the suicide. It is often a projection of shame, guilt and anger."[14] Finally, escape from reality is not only at the foundation of all kinds of neuroses, but also risks making the life of suicide survivors into something pathological, even leading them to commit or attempt suicide as a way of avoiding shame and embarrassment. Therefore, according to Gyulay, "The anger at the dead person is often then turned in toward one's self, causing depression. The depression, shame, and guilt can lead to suicide."[15] Nevertheless, as pointed out above, according to Dunn and Morrish-Vidners, when suicide survivors are able to challenge themselves openly, honestly and without denying reality, they can have access to more integrated lives characterized by a greater sense of wholeness and fulfillment. Even if the reasons for suicide, as will be emphasized later on, can remain forever incomprehensible, suicide can bring about new insights, enabling a better understanding of old patterns of behavior. It can also help suicide survivors to discover how dysfunctional their relationships may have been. As a result, suicide can, ironically, lead suicide survivors to a more integrated way of being and living.

In the bereavement process, Reed and Greenwald underline how parent survivors of children or adolescents who commit suicide are particularly vulnerable to guilt, shame, rejection, self-blame and being blamed by others:

> Parents have the responsibility for the growth and protection of their children. When a child commits suicide or when a child's accidental death results from the lack of parental supervision or control, the competency and credibility of the parents are questioned. The parents may view themselves and/or be considered by others as failures or as "bad" parents. . . . Feelings of blame, guilt, and stigma, and separation pain . . . as well as outward expressions of grief such as angry outbursts and excessive crying are prominent reactions of parents to the death of their child.[16]

Nevertheless, these authors emphasize that suicide can become a kind of blessing for survivors: "Further, qualitative responses to open-ended questions strongly suggest that some family members welcomed the suicide as a blessing, a relief from years of anguish caused by the decedent's drug abuse, spouse and child abuse, marital discord, and mental illness."[17] When families have been constantly threatened, or ashamed by one person's actions, the suicide of this person can become a real liberation for survivors, at least at the beginning of the bereavement process.

No one is in a better position than a suicide survivor to describe the feelings and emotions that survivors experience in the bereavement process. Alison Wertheimer, a survivor of her only sister's suicide in 1979, narrates beautifully the experiences through which some survivors pass. Besides the points that I have already noted regarding the taboo surrounding suicide, Wertheimer underlines another dimension which is always present in the experience of shame: the pain and suffering of feeling publicly exposed. "Once more," she says, "their private tragedy becomes exposed to a wider audience; inquests take place in public – 'justice must be seen to be done' – and anyone is entitled to walk in off the street and sit in the coroner's court."[18] Survivors have the tendency to consider suicide a taboo and may even go so far as never again to mention the person's name. In doing so, "family myths or secrets may be created where the truth becomes denied or distorted as families attempt to avoid their feelings of guilt and the pain of their loss."[19] For Wertheimer, too, bereavement through suicide increases the stress associated with any kind of death. Gyulay indicates how suicide challenges the overall dynamic of what goes on in the family and thus causes many to remain silent about a suicide. So also, Wertheimer says that "Not talking about the suicide can be a way of not having to face the truth of what happened."[20] Denying the suicide liberates them from being obliged to confront reality.

The results of several studies on suicide survivors appeared in 1992.[21] These authors stress that reactions of fear, anger, aggression, feelings and emotions of embarrassment, blame and shame, along with the sense of less social support and the silence surrounding the circumstances of the death, are all typical experiences among suicide survivors.

The above reactions, feelings, emotions, lack of social support and the silence regarding a suicide also came to light in research on suicide survivors carried out during 1993. For example, Clark, Jones, Quinn, Goldney, and Cooling analyze the role of support groups among survivors and point out how support for people in bereavement is lacking due "to societal attitudes . . . and the fragmentation of family and community networks."[22] Heikkinen et al. highlight the risk of suicide and suicide attempt among survivors as an escapist way of coping with the painful feelings and emotions in the aftermath of a suicide.[23] Reed investigates what is specific to and has a long-term effect on coping with suicide by survivors versus what characterizes coping by survivors of other kinds of death.[24] Trolley describes the feelings of rejection, abandonment, and guilt present among survivors, particularly for parents whose children have died by suicide. He also develops an understanding of other dynamics through which survivor families pass. Family members blame one another; parents are overprotective of the remaining children; and all follow a rule of silence which becomes a sort of norm. These feelings are accentuated by the role that shame plays as an important emotion impairing the bereavement process.[25]

As Valente and Saunders indicate in their research regarding adolescent grief after suicide, "parents who are ashamed of suicide may go so far as to deny the facts of suicide, ignore the adolescent's grief, or pretend nothing happened."[26] Together with anger, guilt, depression, shame, denial, and so forth, Van Dongen adds that "a search for meaning [has] been described as [a] common [reaction] associated with grief postsuicide."[27] In reality, very often survivors will never arrive at a full understanding of the reasons the person had for committing this final and lethal act. As a result, during the bereavement process survivors should be told not to expect, now or in the future, an answer to every rational question. Not trying to understand everything can serve as the beginning of a deeper way of healing. It may then finally be possible to let go of the need to find a fully rational explanation for every aspect of a question and of the idea that one can arrive at a better contact with one's innermost feelings and emotions through such an emphasis on intellectualizing the experience.

The response of the social network appears to be, according to Allen, Calhoun, Cann, and Tedeschi, one of the most significant differences between suicide survivors and survivors of other kinds of death. According to these authors, Western culture's "general attitudes toward suicide are negative. There are moral proscriptions against suicide and although suicidal actions are more acceptable under some circumstances, suicide is generally viewed as an undesirable and abnormal act."[28] As a conclusion to their research, Allen et al. reaffirm what other researchers have already emphasized regarding the bereavement process among suicide survivors.

As a result of their research on bereavement from suicide as compared to other forms of bereavement, Silverman, Range, and Overholser indicate that "The suicidally bereaved group reported higher levels of General Grief, Loss of Social Support, Stigmatization, Responsibility, Rejection, Self-Destructive Behavior, and Unique Reactions as compared to each of the other four bereavement groups [homicide, accidental death, natural anticipated death, and natural unanticipated death]. The suicide group also experienced more Shame than the accident and homicide groups."[29] In addition, two studies in 1995 emphasize in a particular way the important role of shame in relation to stigma. For Clark and Goldney, who researched grief reactions and recovery in a support group for people bereaved by suicide, "Many group members experienced a sense of shame which they regarded as a unique burden to suicide bereavement. . . . Other causes of shame included guilt and rejection and being subjects of gossip. Many had difficulty in revealing the cause of death to others, and this often led to long-term deception."[30] However, the research done by Séguin, Lesage, and Kiely, comparing parental bereavement after suicide and after an accident, underlines still more the specific character of the role of shame in relation to suicide survivors, as well as the unique experience they have, compared with survivors of other deaths. According to these authors,

> Less attention has been paid to shame as being a troubling affect that interfaces psychological experience with social stigma associated with a suicide death. . . . Shame is often linked with humiliation, whereas guilt is defined as involving responsibility for an event or a feeling of culpability. In this perspective, shame plays an important social role and could intensify the stigma associated to suicide bereavement.[31]

Shame

One important dimension to consider here is the fact that stigma is intensified by shame. I am convinced that not only is the stigma attached to suicide responsible for shame reactions, but this stigma itself is the result of shame. In fact, one of the hypotheses of Séguin et al., subsequently supported by their research, was "that shame would characterize the uniqueness of suicide bereavement."[32] Thus,

Shame seems to be unique and central to the experience of suicide bereavement, as confirmed by the fact that it shows a clear difference at nine months. Because this affect is an important part of the grief experience, it may in some circumstances interfere with the way survivors of suicide interact with other people, and the manner in which social support is offered to them. Almost all of the parents have the impression that they failed in some way, thus putting their parental competency into question. Survivors feel awkward within their families and with friends. They no longer feel that they are competent providers for the rest of the family. This feeling is extremely distressing and hurtful, and it creates dissonance in their concept of self by bringing to the forefront actions or attitudes that are inconsistent with their own idea of who they are or who they ought to be. This may explain why survivors of suicide complain of low social support even if, quantitatively, social support is present and offered. Survivors tend to isolate themselves more than other bereaved, thus making it hard for family and friends to give support. In turn, the survivors do not perceive their family as potential supporters, thus creating an even larger sense of isolation. There might be a feedback loop between social and psychological dimensions that is extremely important in suicide bereavement.[33]

This is an excellent summary of the important role that shame plays in the lives and coping mechanisms of suicide survivors. It seems to me necessary here to underscore further what these authors say regarding social support. So far, most research done on suicide survivors highlights how social support is less present in the bereavement process of deaths by suicide. However, Séguin et al. stress that shame makes it difficult, if not impossible, for people to take advantage of the social support which is available. In other words, shame vitiates the process of having a more objective perception of reality. This corroborates my observations in chapter two on how shame impairs the cognitive perception of reality.

In their research regarding family interactions of suicide survivors compared with interactions among survivors of non-suicidal death, Nelson and Frantz describe how the entire family system is affected by the emotions of shame and guilt that suicide generates:

Family myths are often constructed to conceal suicide in order to mask the shame and guilt; this in turn compounds deviant grief reactions. Suicide seems to challenge the family's entire belief system including their own sense of themselves as a unit. The ritual of secrecy about the death and the lack of open communication often result in interminable mourning.[34]

Families, relatives, and friends are not the only ones affected by suicide. Therapists, practitioners and mental health professionals also become suicide survivors when one of their clients or patients commits suicide.[35] Grad et al., researching gender differences in bereavement reactions of therapists, point out that "the most marked gender difference in feelings after the suicide was shame."[36] Women admitted to it more frequently than men. Furthermore, in their research on the effects of suicide on the private practitioner, Fox and Cooper report on shame arising as a result of feeling a sense of failure at being unable to prevent a client from committing suicide.[37]

From 1999 to 2003, further interesting research has been done on suicide survivors and the bereavement process. Even while they recognize that suicide survivors do not form a homogeneous group, Bailley, Kral, and Dunham emphasize the components of the bereavement process characteristic of these groups.[38] Shame, embarrassment, stigma, secrecy, sadness, self-accusation, psychopathological symptoms, feelings of rejection, and even the risk of attempting or committing suicide, particularly in older people, are, once more, documented as part of the experience of suicide survivors.

I have found two pieces of research that do not support the majority of research results. One of these was done by Murphy, Johnson, Wu, Fan, and Lohan,[39] and the other by Murphy, Tapper, Johnson, and Lohan.[40] These scholars studied whether there are any differences between parents surviving the death of a child caused by violence such as accident or homicide, and parents surviving the suicide of a child. According to Murphy, Johnson, Wu, Fan, and Lohan, "Contrary to established belief, a child's death by suicide did not contribute to parents' highest levels of distress and the lowest levels of acceptance of the deaths, or marital satisfaction, when compared with parents bereaved by accident and homicide. Moreover, the findings showed that changes in outcomes over time is an important factor."[41] Furthermore, Murphy, Tapper, Johnson, and Lohan write: "One finding that differs from long-standing 'conventional wisdom' is that the suicidal death of a child did not result in the highest rates of SI [Suicidal Ideation] among the parents. Rather, higher percentages of parents reporting SI occurred among those bereaved by accidental and homicidal deaths."[42] However, these findings do not reflect the generalized common experience of parent survivors of children who die by suicide, or survivors of suicide in general, as I have thus far presented it here.

Finally, according to the majority of research done in this field, one particular aspect of the question we are studying regarding the relationship between shame and suicide survivors appears to be essential: the relationship between shame and stigma. I now wish to focus on this in a special way.

Suicide and Social Image

What Victoria Alexander says regarding suicide survivors' feelings and emotions, and concerning societal attitudes toward suicide seems obvious to me: "Fortunately, we no longer punish suicide so severely, but the secrecy, silence, and shame remain with the survivors, along with our discomfort as a society."[43] Suicide is still considered a stigmatized and stigmatizing event in our society. Additionally, as indicated previously, I believe that before being a source of shame, stigma is a consequence of it; shame assures that suicide bears a stigma. However, once that stigma has been attached to it, suicide, already considered as a stigmatized event, itself becomes a source of shame. The stigmatization of suicide by society, culture and religion, and the relationship between shame and stigma, act as an environmental constraint against coping with suicide in a healthy way during the bereavement process.

In his research on the bereaved and the stigma of suicide, Mark I. Solomon describes the ancient and modern usage of stigma: "In ancient Greece a stigma was a mark burned into the skin that signified that its bearer was a criminal or slave. In modern usage, the term has been broadened to mean a mark of shame or disgrace, whether visible or not, that potentially detracts from the character or reputation of a person."[44] What makes this stigmatization so negative an experience is its link with shame or disgrace. In fact, it is the "mark of shame or disgrace" that causes stigma to be considered an infamy. It is well known that, as the Bible frequently narrates, the leper and people afflicted by other visible diseases had to remain separate from the community, to dress in a particular way, and to announce their presence from a distance in order to avoid making healthy people unclean through contact with them (Leviticus 13–14; Luke 17:11–14). More recently, we can think of the shame and humiliation that Jewish people experienced in some European countries during World War II (1939–1945), when they were forced to live in ghettoes and concentration camps, and to wear a mark on their clothes (a stigma) that disclosed publicly their own cultural and religious identity to an adverse society.

From a socio-cultural perspective, people outside the family have the tendency to stigmatize survivors of suicide, particularly when survivors are parents of adolescent suicides.[45] Thus, according to Dunn and Morrish-Vidners,

> suicide bereavement is shaped by the difficult task of adjusting emotionally and personally to an anomalous and tragic event. This task is further complicated by the social stigma surrounding suicide and the resulting uncertainty, confusion, and awkwardness of others' reactions. Recovery from this type of loss thus threatens to be delayed by numerous emotional and social impediments faced by the survivors.[46]

Nevertheless, among suicide survivors, grief reactions generated by stigma are different, according to McIntosh and Wrobleski:

> Stigma-related events were reported by survivors of all kinship relations, and while guilt and avoiding talking about the deceased on the part of others seem to be common

elements, there were to some degree differences in the stigma experienced. More specifically, siblings and spouses, and to a lesser degree parents whose young children committed
suicide, may experience greater amounts of social stigmatizing in their interactions with
others.[47]

Why parent survivors of suicide are more stigmatized by others has already
been indicated above in the second part of this chapter. In particular, Reed and
Greenwald underlined that the fact of having responsibility for their children
makes parents more vulnerable to criticism by others for not having provided
their children with the expected support. This also means that such parents
appear to have failed in their parental role.

Stigma and Shame

How stigma is a source of shame can be deduced, too, from the research done
by Gyulay. "Suicide is not a socially acceptable act by most societal and religious
standards. In recent years, suicide has been less stigmatizing, however, families
often project their feelings of shame. They may live for years feeling that everyone
is pointing a finger at the stigma of a loved one who committed suicide."[48] In
fact, according to Clemons, who develops some attitudes toward suicide from a
historical perspective,

> The extreme social [cultural and religious] stigma against suicide had reached its height in
> the Middle Ages. There was punishment for those who attempted it, public desecration
> of the corpses of those who committed it, and loss of inheritance and continuing social
> pressures for family survivors. (Today, stigma is generally regarded by suicidologists as
> both a reason for people not seeking the help they need to prevent suicide, as well as un
> unjust and often cruel form of punishment against innocent survivors.)[49]

This expresses well how stigma acts as an environmental constraint against
survivors' coping with suicide in a positive way. For this, "Normal avenues of
grief support and facilitation from family, friends, and the community are often
severed in a suicide death. . . . It has been suggested that the survivors of suicide
death feel that they are living a stigmatized life, and are no longer able to be open
with their feelings."[50] It is, then, understandable that suicide survivors, rather than
feel stigmatized by others, would prefer to remain silent about the circumstances
of the death, even though this attitude will lead to dysfunctional behaviors.

In the previously cited research done by Clark and Goldney regarding grief
reactions and recovery in a support group for people bereaved by suicide, survivors experience stigma, together with the presence of shame: "They [many group
members] felt stigma from the previous illegal status of suicide, which ended
in 1983 in South Australia, the churches' current and previous attitudes, the

association between suicide and mental illness, tainting of the family tree, or from a belief in a supernatural evil power acting on the family."[51] Thus, survivors consider suicide to be a sort of curse that has negative consequences on them.

Séguin et al. also relate shame with stigma when they point out that "Less attention has been paid to shame as being a troubling affect that interfaces psychological experience with social stigma associated with a suicide death."[52] In the same vein, shame, together with stigmatization and embarrassment, is what distinguishes suicide survivors from survivors of death from other causes: "Survivors have often been characterized as experiencing stigmatization, social isolation, and strained relationships."[53] Jaques stresses that "Suicide, with its connotations of societal taboo, heightens the level of difficulty for consideration of loss and grief among family members."[54]

In addition, two research studies done in 2001 regarding the specific character of the bereavement process of deaths by suicide emphasize the role of stigma on survivors. Jordan points out that "there is considerable evidence that the general stigma that continues to be associated with suicide in our society 'spills over' to the bereaved family members."[55] Furthermore, Selakovic-Bursic says that "Despite the fact that suicide is a relatively frequent phenomenon in the area [Novi Sad, Hungary], it is rarely discussed and leaves a social stigma upon the surviving family. When obituaries for suicide victims appear in local papers, the word suicide is never mentioned."[56] Consequently, the stigmatization of suicide is not something exclusive to North American society.

Finally, even taking into account how the attitudes of the majority of religious denominations and churches regarding suicide have changed, we cannot say that the stigma attached by previous religious views about suicide has disappeared. The fact is that until quite recently suicide was considered a grave sin, was condemned by churches, and was the reason for denying religious burial to those who committed suicide. This former practice continues to have a stigmatizing effect on survivors.

Conclusion

During the past decade, one of the most important dimensions of research on suicide was research's focus on the bereavement process of survivors. However, my intention in this chapter has been to underline more specifically the particular link between shame and suicide survivors. In fact, I consider shame to be a personal and environmental constraint that makes it difficult for survivors to cope with suicide in a positive manner.

First, this chapter dealt with those who attempt unsuccessful suicides. These people have to deal not only with the shame and stigma engendered by their near deadly attempt, but they also frequently find themselves in a situation that becomes so painful that they risk trying again to commit suicide in order to liberate themselves from their feelings of shame and the stigma attached to the first attempt. Second, shame impairs the bereavement process of survivors in many ways. Survivors may even try to deny the reality of the suicide in order to avoid their uncomfortable situation. However, suicide survivors can also move ahead in a more integrated way if they are able and willing to accept the fact of the suicide and work through their relationship to it. Third, in spite of some new ways of understanding suicide, it still carries a certain stigma from a socio-cultural and religious perspective. This makes the bereavement process much more difficult, if not impossible, for some survivors.

One of the main purposes of the present study is to contribute to overcoming the dysfunctional influences of chronic shame on suicide in order to help people cope with it in a healthier way. The following chapter deals with this liberating task.

Notes

[1]   Yufit, 1991, p. 152.
[2]   Yufit, 1991, p. 153.
[3]   Yufit, 1991, p. 163.
[4]   Alexander, 1991, p. 278.
[5]   Tejedor, Díaz, Castillón, & Pericay, 1999, p. 210.
[6]   Tejedor et al., 1999, p. 205.
[7]   Tejedor et al., 1999, p. 210.
[8]   Rowe, 1991, p. 262.
[9]   Dunn & Morrish-Vidners, 1987–88, p. 176.
[10] Calhoun & Allen, 1991; Mauk & Weber, 1991; Parkes, 1985.
[11] Barret & Scott, 1989, p. 205.
[12] Gyulay, 1989, p. 105.
[13] Gyulay, 1989, p. 110.
[14] Gyulay, 1989, p. 113.
[15] Gyulay, 1989, p. 117.
[16] Reed & Greenwald, 1991, pp. 388–389.
[17] Reed & Greenwald, 1991, pp. 398–399.
[18] Wertheimer, 1991, p. 21.
[19] Wertheimer, 1991, p. 23.
[20] Wertheimer, 1991, p. 112.
[21] Farberow, Gallagher-Thompson, Gilewski, & Thompson, 1992a; Farberow, Gallagher-Thompson, Gilewski, & Thompson, 1992b; McIntosh & Kelly, 1992; Tekavcic-Grad & Zavasnik, 1992; Thompson & Range, 1992.
[22] Clark, Jones, Quinn, Goldney, & Cooling, 1993, p. 161.
[23] Heikkinen et al., 1993.
[24] Reed, 1993.
[25] Trolley, 1993.
[26] Valente & Saunders, 1993, p. 17.
[27] Van Dongen, 1993, p. 125.
[28] Allen, Calhoun, Cann, & Tedeschi, 1993–94, p. 40.
[29] Silverman, Range, & Overholser, 1994–95, p. 45. Upper case in the original text.
[30] Clark & Goldney, 1995, p. 30.
[31] Séguin, Lesage, & Kiely, 1995, p. 489.
[32] Séguin et al., 1995, p. 490.
[33] Séguin et al., 1995, p. 495.
[34] Nelson & Frantz, 1996, p. 132.
[35] Thomas, 2003.
[36] Grad, Zavasnik, & Groleger, 1997, p. 384.
[37] Fox & Cooper, 1998.

[38]   Bailley, Kral, & Dunham, 1999.

[39]   Murphy, Johnson, Wu, Fan, & Lohan, 2003.

[40]   Murphy, Tapper, Johnson, & Lohan, 2003.

[41]   Murphy, Johnson, Wu, Fan, & Lohan, 2003, p. 54.

[42]   Murphy, Tapper, Johnson, & Lohan, 2003, p. 19.

[43]   Alexander, 1991, p. 280.

[44]   Solomon, 1982–83, p. 377.

[45]   Godney, Spence, & Moffitt, 1987.

[46]   Dunn & Morrish-Vidners, 1987–88, p. 176.

[47]   McIntosh & Wrobleski, 1988, p. 36.

[48]   Gyulay, 1989, p. 116.

[49]   Clemons, 1990, p. 81.

[50]   Mauk & Weber, 1991, p. 115.

[51]   Clark & Goldney, 1995, p. 30.

[52]   Séguin et al., 1995, p. 489.

[53]   Knieper, 1999, p. 356.

[54]   Jaques, 2000, p. 377.

[55]   Jordan, 2001, p. 93.

[56]   Selakovic-Bursic, 2001, p. 47.

Chapter V

Shame as Cause or Consequence of Suicide

Chronic shame plays a very negative role in the overall span and development of one's life. This occurs in a particular way when people confront life's stressful experiences. Shame spoils the cognitive perception of reality and hence of the self in such a way that one who experiences shame risks becoming alienated not only from others, but also from one's own self. The resulting isolation vitiates the process of coping with difficulties, leading to an inability to share with others one's innermost, and usually painful, feelings and emotions. As shown in previous chapters, the consequences can be deadly. Furthermore, shame is not only increased by the fact that suicide is considered to be an event that carries with it a stigma. Shame itself can be at the source of stigmatization, that is, it can itself contribute to suicide as a social, cultural and religious stigma. This occurs especially in the bereavement process of survivors.

Thus, if we take into serious consideration what Yufit stresses regarding suicide prevention, as it has been addressed in the last chapter, we see that educational programs for helping adolescents, parents, educators and adults gradually acquire healthier skills to cope with stress, must give special attention to the devastating role that shame has in suicide and suicide-related events. This special attention must also be given by those working with clinical assessment techniques for determining who is at risk of suicide. In this regard, it seems important to me to expand not only school programs for educating youth and parents to cope better with stress, but also to help people become reconciled with their own selves. I shall develop this idea in the first part of this chapter. To become reconciled with one's own self is a process in which one recognizes and accepts that dysfunction, vulnerability and fragility are essential dimensions of being human. Furthermore, I believe that only when one is reconciled with the humanness of one's own being can one then share innermost feelings and emotions with others. The second part of the present chapter will highlight how this requires that one be sufficiently secure in one's awareness and appreciation of one's self in order to be able to disclose one's self to others. Finally, the third part of this chapter will emphasize that becoming reconciled with one's self and being able to share innermost feelings and emotions with others is interconnected with the transformation of social, cultural and religious attitudes toward suicide.

In this chapter I shall present my own reflections on how to overcome the negative relationship between shame and suicide, taking into account all the research analyzed thus far. The three points that this chapter will develop correspond to what I consider the most important dimensions that must be identified in order to overcome the problem that binds chronic shame and suicide.

Reconciling the Self

The aim of human development is to become a free, autonomous, responsible person, one who is able to establish a network of satisfying and healthy relationships with others. However, human growth does not happen in the abstract. From infancy to late adulthood, human beings develop within a particular environment, within historical, cultural, economic, social, political and religious contexts that condition, in one way or another, the manner in which a person grows up. One's lifespan is also influenced by race, gender and ethnic origins. Today, in North American society, and in Western society in general, people develop in a pluralistic, multicultural milieu which challenges more traditional, defined ways of being educated. Human development is also conditioned by genetic, hereditary factors.[1]

Nevertheless, there are particular experiences that damage the dynamic of maturation. These can arise from interaction with the environment, from other people's behavior, and from heredity.[2] In this sense, and following what I have presented thus far in this study, one can say that chronic shame is one of the most negative factors that impair human growth in many different ways. It impedes development toward maturity and toward becoming fully human and alive.

As we saw in the first chapter, shame occurs when one feels one has failed in a particular role, when one's performance is measured against the standard established by the ego-ideal self. Then, one believes oneself to be exposed to others. One assumes that one's weaknesses and limitations are disclosed to the invasive glare of others, particularly to others who are very important to oneself. Therefore, feeling a personal failure, and anticipating, even in an imagined way, the reaction of significant others leads the shame-prone person to experience stress and a loss of self-esteem. Finally, the consequences of shame manifest themselves in the desire to disappear, in feeling unworthy, in a lack of intimacy not only with others but also with the self. At the end, one finishes by protecting oneself not only from others, but also from one self. One develops a false identity.

In this sense, a first step in the therapeutic process of addressing shame means that psychologists and health professionals must help clients to recognize and accept shame in their lives. Only then will they be able to succeed in overcoming shame's negative influence. Thus, according to Warren Breed,

> What the other person—professional or layman—must do is to help the patient in his ability to *cope with crisis*. In some cases the "failure" is illusory, and the wise helper can point this out, thus reducing shame and isolation. The helper can also counsel experimentation with *switching goals, roles, and social contacts,* and a reduction in commitment (placing the eggs in different baskets).[3]

Becoming reconciled with one's own self, which is the royal way to a fulfilled life, requires that we start with the recognition and the acceptance of our own alienations and vulnerabilities, and our own constitutional fragility in growing to maturity. Besides, fragility and vulnerability are essential dimensions of being human. The desire to be perfect (i.e., the perfectionism that urges us to perform and excel at any cost) can become a pathological manifestation of an uninte-grated person. What I say regarding this desire to be perfect applies as well to our attitudes toward limits and imperfections found in others, in nature, in socio-cultural, political and religious structures, and in the world in general. Further-more, becoming reconciled with one's own self leads to openness to others. Thus, according to Goldberg, who presents a guide to the healing of shame,

> Adult shame has at its roots the feelings of abandonment by caretakers in the patient's past. To undo shame, attachment to compassionate figures needs to be regained or, per-haps even for the first time, secured. Overcoming shame is best achieved in a trusted and intimate relationship in which the therapist is a fellow sojourner, able to be emotionally touched by the patient, rather than being an objective expert interested in an archeological quest of mummified demons.[4]

Becoming reconciled with one's self, which also implies the ability to be intimate with one's self, makes it possible for us to develop intimate relationships with others, to manifest hospitality, and to become compassionate beings. However, it is extremely difficult to develop "attachment to compassionate figures" when one is divided within oneself. For this reason, overcoming the consequences of shame is better done in a therapeutic milieu. There, the therapist or counselor can play the role of a "significant other" in the life of the client while at the same time helping the client to reconstruct her or his self. In this way, one can develop a stronger self-concept and self-esteem that will facilitate one's reconciliation with one's own self, and will nurture one's capacity for openness to others.

In summary, when one is better prepared to accept one's own self in a realistic way, that is, when one assumes one's own constitutive limits, namely, the imperfections, weaknesses and so forth that one experiences in oneself and in life, one is better able to open oneself to others. This helps overcome or at least significantly diminish the risk that suicide and attempted suicide will be used as a way to cope with shameful and difficult situations.

Sharing Unspeakable Feelings

Another essential dimension in human development is the ability to share one's innermost feelings and emotions with others. We cannot pretend that others are gods or goddesses who can easily discover on their own what we are feeling and experiencing. Consequently, one of the most important tasks in suicide prevention consists in helping people to develop healthy communication skills. That will help them to cope with shame, particularly in its relationship to suicide. As Apter et al. emphasize,

> An impaired ability for self-disclosure has also been found to increase isolation and the degree of loneliness and suffering. . . . Loneliness has also been empirically shown to be related to the lack of self-disclosure. . . . An intimate partner is also important for the correction of negative perceptions people may have of themselves and their environment and may attenuate of negative emotions such as depression, anxiety and anger, which are themselves important facilitators of suicidal behavior.[5]

Chronic shame leads to secrecy and social isolation. Thus, to prevent a shame-prone person from becoming a stranger to himself or herself, and to overcome the negative consequences of shame such as suicide and attempted suicide, it is important to develop healthy interactions, that is, genuine friendships with significant others with whom we are able to communicate. Furthermore, we need to be able to talk in a free way especially about the most stressful and disturbing events in our lives

Nevertheless, there are three pitfalls to be avoided, three factors that can impair the process of openness to others. First, as indicated in Chapter I, one has to consider the lack, at least until recently, of scientific language with which to express feelings and emotions, namely, inner experiences.[6]

The second factor is the extreme sense of privacy in North American culture that impedes self-disclosure. The difficulty people have in expressing inner experiences is due not only to the lack of scientific language, but also to a cultural prejudice, what I call the taboo of privacy in North American society. A healthier and less extreme sense of privacy is very different from what can be called "savage subjectivism," or the tendency to consider oneself as the only point of reference for everything. Likewise, it is different from being closed to others in the sense of being unable to share what one feels and believes, or being concerned only with one's own life in a very individualistic way. Privacy, like *modesty*, is not opposed to otherness. On the contrary, privacy is the respect for one's own intimacy and its protection from an invasion by others and, oftentimes, from their morbid curiosity.[7]

A healthy sense of privacy does not keep human beings from setting up a network of relationships. Indeed, people can discover their gifts, their talents, and who they are in the eyes of those who recognize and receive them, particularly in the eyes of those who love them.[8] Only in the presence of another human being can people discover themselves as human, as Adam did in the presence of Eve, according to one of the two symbolic creation stories of the biblical book of Genesis (Gn 2:23). Others are not potential enemies, but people who reflect, as in a mirror, one's own self. This mirroring from others is essential for human development.[9] It permits one to share one's innermost feelings and emotions with someone else.

The third pitfall in the process of openness to others refers to the lack of communication skills as such. People used to believe that the simple fact that they were able to speak meant they could communicate, that is, share feelings and emotions. However, this is frequently not true. Often, rather than sharing, people make accusations against one another. They block the process of communication, and put the other person on the defensive. Teaching people techniques for communicating in a mature way, without accusing or degrading others, is an essential element in the effort to overcome the influences of pathological shame, to resolve stressful situations and, in other words, to forestall those painful experiences leading persons toward attempted suicidal behavior.

In the second and fourth chapters I spoke of the relationship between shame, social isolation and suicide, including the bereavement process of survivors. We know that social isolation can be the fruit of a distorted perception of reality, and may not necessarily be due to the attitudes of others. Accordingly, the only way of overcoming this confusion is by learning to share one's own needs and dysfunctions in an explicit and unambiguous way.

Finally, it will be necessary to develop improved assessment techniques and expanded educational programs at all levels. This will enable people to acquire skills in both communication and problem-solving in order to deal in particular with such stressful events as chronic shame. It will also improve the manner whereby survivors cope with the aftermath of suicide and will become an excellent approach to overcoming shame both as a cause and a consequence of suicide. However, it will not be possible to succeed in this endeavor unless a direction is taken toward the transformation of all social, cultural and religious attitudes toward suicide itself.

Healing Attitudes on Suicide: Culture and Religion

Various sciences have helped us to understand suicide better. As a consequence, religious attitudes regarding suicide are not as condemnatory and negative as they once were. Nevertheless, we have also seen that suicide is, from a socio-cultural and religious perspective, still largely considered a stigmatized event. In fact, cultural attitudes regarding an event like suicide do not change very rapidly, even if the laws dealing with such an event may have changed. For this reason, transforming socio-cultural and religious attitudes regarding suicide, particularly the stigmatization attached to it, remains an essential element in the development of school programs for coping with suicide and suicide-related events, in social interventions with families and people at high risk, in pastoral approaches dealing with suicide, and in faculties of medicine. It is important to help physicians acquire a better understanding of the complexities of suicidal behavior, as well as of the dynamics of the bereavement process of survivors. In fact, physicians must acquire a more holistic understanding of death and dying.

Speaking about the psychological and social experiences of suicide survivors, Dunn and Morrish-Vidners address the importance of death education in order to overcome some of the problems, such as stigma, that suicide survivors experience. They conclude:

> We argue, however, that the social needs of suicide survivors are primarily the responsibility of educators. While death education is extremely helpful, an ability to reflect on suicide as a moral and philosophical problem is a necessary precondition for overcoming the stigma and moral void pervading the situation of survivors. Beyond these intellectual tasks, we believe that many of the problems faced by survivors result from a lack of education in the emotions and could be lessened by major efforts in the areas of early childhood socialization, adolescent schooling, counseling, therapy, and other areas where members of society can be taught to relate to each other in more humane and emotionally sensitive ways.[10]

Efforts to deal with the philosophical and moral problems of suicide must, of necessity, be made through education. This is true not only for those experiencing stressful events in their lives, but also for the general population. Wertheimer, in her testimony as a survivor of suicide, emphasizes the important role religion may play in helping people to overcome the stigma of suicide. She says, "Members of the clergy are frequently in contact with a bereaved family immediately after the death and are, therefore, a potentially important source of support to survivors.

Like anyone else, though, clergy may have difficulty in coming to terms with their own feelings about suicide."[11] What Wertheimer emphasizes regarding the role of clergy is true. Of course, in order to accomplish such a task, ministers themselves need to have an enlightened understanding of suicide, and of death and dying in general, and must overcome their own prejudices regarding it. Furthermore, Wertheimer indicates that,

> The funeral can fulfil several other important functions [besides the fact of allowing survivors to do something for the deceased]: it can bring together a network of people to express their support for the bereaved relatives . . . and acknowledge their own sense of loss; it allows the bereaved to experience the full reality of the death . . . and the ritual of the funeral enacts a separation of the living from the dead. . . . All these functions are important for survivors of suicide, and some particularly so. In cases of suicide, survivors have often not seen the body; the funeral may be the first (and only) time they come face to face with the reality of death by seeing the coffin, and by hearing publicly words of farewell.[12]

Saying Goodbye

Funerals, then, can become an extremely important way of educating people in order to acquire a different, less stigmatized, view of suicide. These liturgies can also challenge one of the difficulties that I find in Western (North American) society regarding death in general: considering death as a shameful aspect of life. Death and dying, like many other important experiences of loss in human life, are not necessarily shameful events in and of themselves, nor have they always been so experienced in the past. However, in today's Western society generally, and not only in shame-prone individuals, families and relationships, it has become difficult to deal with death, dying and the process of bereavement. Faced with these existential experiences, people feel ashamed to express their innermost feelings and emotions; they hide, deny, repress or cover them up.[13]

Death and dying have become a shameful aspect of life.[14] The taboo of sex that characterized Western society during the nineteenth century, particularly in Victorian England and, through its influence, in North America, has been replaced by the taboo of death and dying.[15] Toward the second half of the last century, death, which until then had been a faithful companion of human life, became a reality that is more and more the subject of denial. Not long ago, death and dying belonged to the essence of life. To be born and to die were two essential dimensions of every family experience, as these events usually happened at home. Today, Western society's attitudes toward death and dying have undergone a great transformation. Death has become the last neurosis of life,[16] and the dying person is virtually denied the possibility of integrating her or his own death as the last stage of life. To refuse reality, particularly the tendency to deny unpleasant events, is at the heart of all neurosis. In this sense, as Parsons highlights,

> Americans are allegedly coming to be progressively less capable of facing the harsh realities of the actual world. Unpleasant things tend to be regarded as not very "real." We are said to live in a kind of world of illusion; to construct an elaborate system of defenses to protect ourselves against the intrusion of reality into this world. The problem of death becomes only one, though a particularly striking, manifestation of this general tendency.[17]

Even the dying person enters into this process of denial. This is the result of silencing one's innermost feelings and emotions, as well as the concern for privacy in present-day North American society, as I have already indicated. Death and dying have become a private matter.[18]

People also perceive the process of dying as shameful because of the dying person's isolation from significant others. For a dying person, significant others include not only members of that person's family, but also those to whose care he or she is entrusted, such as health professionals and staff. Thus, if one of the sources in the development of shame is the break-up of relationships with significant others, we can readily understand why the experience of dying becomes so shameful. "The effect, once again, of such avoidance is that the human community abandons, and thereby breaks faith with, the dying person."[19] The dying person feels diminished as a human being, humiliated for feeling so vulnerable and being so dependent on others. He or she is even tempted to embark upon a process of denial of her or his real situation. At the same time, significant others feel embarrassed in his or her presence. These feelings themselves reveal a certain sense of shame. Furthermore, one of the consequences of dying in the hospital, and, in some cases, of the "quick, closed-coffin funerals and 'clean' cremations,"[20] is the complexification or suppression of the process of mourning by considering it shameful. Today,

> [many] deaths in the United States occur outside of the home. Many die within the impersonal confines of a hospital or nursing home. Because of this, the healing process of those close to the deceased is negatively affected. Various thanatological authorities conclude that in the bereavement process, much of the effectiveness of this process depends upon the recognition of the reality of the death by the mourners. Much of this reality is lost when families cannot experience the death process simply because it occurs away from home.[21]

Nevertheless, the only way in which people can live a full life is by accepting mortality and death as an integral dimension of being human. Thus, it is important to learn from childhood how to integrate death, dying and grieving into one's human development and to challenge some current prevailing attitudes. One has to recognize the important contribution made in this field by Elisabeth Kübler-Ross and others,[22] who argue that death must be considered as the last stage of human development, and dying as a dignified process. Human beings then are expected to appropriate their death and dying to themselves and be able and willing to share the feelings and emotions generated by these important experiences with those with whom they enjoy meaningful relationships. In addition, to be human is to be contingent, that is, mortal. Death and dying indeed are not shameful *stigmas* to be hidden away.

Consequently, changing attitudes toward death and dying challenge the bias of considering death and dying the ultimate manifestation of a failure, either from a personal or a medical perspective. These changing attitudes help us to consider death and dying as the only way through which human beings acquire the fullness of life. In a particular way, as Provini et al. highlight regarding adults mourning suicide, we need to challenge our attitudes on suicide, in order to stop considering it a stigmatized and stigmatizing event. As one of the implications of their research, these authors say:

> ... the current study warrants increased public funding for the study and servicing of the suicidally bereaved population. Public education goals should focus primarily on destigmatizing suicide and informing community members about the unique needs of those impacted by suicide. Educational campaigns must also target service personnel such as mental health professionals, social service workers, primary care physicians, and clergy, in order to facilitate coordination of formal and informal services for the suicidally bereaved, and to refer individuals who may need assistance to appropriate and desired sources of help.[23]

Provini et al. summarize very well what I have been saying about the need to transform social, cultural and religious attitudes on suicide. The shame/suicide relationship, through the process of considering the latter as a stigmatized event, is one of the most destructive that can occur over the course of a life, and needs to be overcome in order for someone to grow up and mature, to become fully human and alive through healthy relationships with others.

Conclusion

The purpose of this chapter has been to help us see how we can overcome shame's role as a cause or as a consequence of suicide. Several factors need to be taken into consideration in order to accomplish this wonderful and noble task. The first factor involves recognizing the importance of being reconciled with one's own self and being open to others. Thus, it seems essential to help people to acquire better problem-solving and communication skills. In this regard, therapy or counseling plays an important role, because the psychologist can become a significant other in the life of the client in order to help him or her not only to develop problem-solving skills, but also to serve as someone with whom the client can learn to communicate in ways that are more mature.

The second important factor in overcoming the unhealthy coupling of shame and suicide is education. We need to educate people from the early stages of life in such a way that they will understand that fragility and vulnerability are essential dimensions of life. We must teach them to cope better with painful, stressful feelings and emotions. Furthermore, schools should integrate programs and studies in their curricula that will lead young people to a more global understanding of death and dying, particularly to a better understanding of the reality of suicide. Thus, every school should develop programs to assess and assist those at high risk of suicide, and to facilitate the bereavement process of student survivors of the suicide of one of their schoolmates, relatives, and friends.

The third factor concerns the importance of socio-cultural, political and religious interventions carried out in order to confront the alarming increase in suicide, and especially to help people overcome the stigmatization surrounding it. In this sense, rather than discouraging speaking about suicide and so contributing to its remaining a taboo, educational campaigns should be organized that will sensitize the general population to the complexities of suicide, particularly among adolescents and the elderly. In addition, more public funding for the prevention of suicide is needed, and more research for studying the negative role of shame in suicide and suicide-related events must be carried out.

Overall, it seems to me that one essential dimension in overcoming shame in its link with suicide consists in being able to speak openly about suicide, without making it a shameful aspect of life, or without being afraid of sharing intimate feelings and emotions with significant others, particularly with regard to the important events that can contribute to fostering a shame-prone personality. There should be no shame in recognizing or accepting someone as a "shamed" person, or that someone has gone through "shameful" experiences such as those of being a suicide survivor or having attempted suicide. Recognition and acceptance are the beginning of our triumph over chronic shame and over the taboo (stigma) surrounding suicide. Thus, it is important to discover, as I narrate in the next chapter, how one becomes empowered by healing.

Notes

1   Gormly & Brodzinsky, 1993.
2   Rosenhan & Seligman, 1995.
3   Breed, 1972, p. 17. Italics in the original text.
4   Goldberg, 1991, p. 263.
5   Apter et al., 2001, pp. 73–74.
6   Kaufman, 1989; Pattison, 2000.
7   Martínez de Pisón, 2002.
8   Chance, 1992; Mokros, 1995; Nouwen, 1975.
9   Feshbach et al., 1996.
10   Dunn & Morrish-Vidners, 1987–88, p. 211.
11   Wertheirmer, 1991, p. 21.
12   Wertheirmer, 1991, p. 22.
13   Harper & Hoopes, 1990.
14   Ariès, 1967, 1974; Bregman, 1999; Parsons, 1963.
15   Ariès, 1967; Christ, 1961; Glaser & Strauss, 1980; Hardt, 1979; Laderman, 2000; Lifton, 1980.
16   Marzouki, 1990.
17   Parsons, 1963, p. 61.
18   Ariès, 1967; Parsons, 1963.
19   Schneider, 1992, p. 85.
20   Woodward, 1970, p. 86.
21   Hardt, 1979, p. 126.
22   Kübler-Ross, 1975, 1978; "Dignity at the end of Life," 2004.
23   Provini, Everett, & Pfeffer, 2000, p. 18.

Chapter VI

Empowered by Healing

In 1972 my father died. His death was called "accidental." However, it was a suspected suicide. Since then, my family has never spoken openly about it. As a matter of fact, in some ways, I believe that his death was considered to be for us a sort of liberation. His being an alcoholic was a source of shame, at least to me. It was difficult to speak with other school children about my father, to share with other people who he was, or even to explain his physical and emotional absence. Nonetheless, I remember feeling that liberation was only temporary. Several years after his death, as an adult, I had to deal with a personal crisis. I had to cope with my own shame, with my relationship with my father, and with his death. Ultimately, I was able to forgive him and become reconciled with his absence in my life. In fact, I missed my father a lot. It was because of this reconciliation that I decided to dedicate to him my second book. I was able to recover his "presence" and his love for me in a different way. Although this was a very difficult experience, I believe it helped me grow and develop in a more mature way.

Healing these painful experiences was the fruit of several years of psychotherapy. In this process I discovered many things. One was the need to recover the memory of these events, of how they affected my growing up in a dysfunctional family, as well as of the dysfunctionality of my own person. I had to learn how to integrate my personal pain into my life as an adult and to transform it in a positive way.

I also discovered how my mother's severity with me during my childhood was her way of avoiding the possibility that I might become like my father. I had to live through the same process of reconciliation with my mother, but I had to do this before she died in order to avoid the difficult experience of becoming reconciled with her only after her departure from this life. This became one of the most liberating experiences of my life: to be able to tell my mother not only how much I suffered but also how much I loved her. For years I had not been able to say to her "Mom I love you!"

In fact, I believe I had been trying all my life to prove that I was not like my father. Perhaps, in some way, this influenced my becoming a Roman Catholic priest and a member of a religious congregation. It allowed me to feel "redeemed" by being present in the lives of others, helping them to give of their very best. Without a doubt, moreover, this was a major motivation for my decision to study psychology and thus gain a better understanding of what I had experienced in my own life in order to contribute to the liberation of others.

However, I also discovered the risk of sliding into a tendency to perfectionism. Perfectionism is a common but painful way of hiding the shame that binds oneself, and, as I indicated in the second chapter, perfectionism can become one of the triggers for suicide attempts. In any case, accepting the fact that "I am not perfect" has had a liberating effect in my life.

The last thing I discovered is that I had a decision to make: either victimize myself, or take my life in my own hands and do something more positive. Facing the risk of victimizing oneself, and recognizing how this tendency is very present in our North American society, I made a commitment to renounce this unhealthy tendency. Victimizing oneself is to surrender our power to others, instead of taking responsibility for our own well-being. In order to experience how empowering the healing process can become, I had to confront what contributed to my tendency to feel ashamed for things for which I was not responsible.

I also remember the stigma attached to suicide. During my childhood and early adolescence, suicide was still considered a grave sin, and Christian burial was denied to those who committed suicide. In my culture of origin, in Southern Spain, we practice a great cult of death. Cemeteries are places where families go to pray, to bring flowers, and to pay tribute to the memory of the deceased. Particularly, in the Roman Catholic tradition, the 2nd of November is devoted to remembering the dead. In a far corner of the cemetery in my own town of Jaén, there was a place popularly called *The Yard of the Hanged* (hanging oneself being the most frequent way of committing suicide in those days). It was a place surrounded by a fence, left more or less unattended by anyone, where those who had committed suicide were interred. I will always remember my fear of approaching this place considered to be "damned." There is no doubt at all that this was the result of the socio-cultural and religious stigma attached to suicide. Furthermore, I was told that in some villages, in order to avoid feeling embarrassed by the situation created by suicide, the priests would sometimes avoid being present at the burial of one who had committed suicide. We can imagine the feelings and emotions of shame, stigma, and the social and religious isolation felt by survivors.

I share here my own experience of becoming empowered by healing, knowing very well that we have erected a taboo regarding our personal feelings and painful experiences. To risk oneself in order to overcome this taboo is an essential part of our journey to freedom. Oftentimes, the suffering of people is not only related to their physical illness or to their psychological distress. Many people suffer because they do not find it possible to share their painful experiences with others. In fact, I believe we can even lose the capacity to name our pain. It seems we always want somehow to feel perfect, great. Unfortunately, reality is not always so simple and easy. To keep silent about these experiences can cause people to become more alienated from themselves and others. Alienation from oneself and from others may induce people to suicide.

Thus, in the first part of this chapter I describe how I deal with my own suffering. I indicate in the second part, that the compassion of others and the compassion of God have been essential to my healing process. This, as I describe it in the last part, allows me to enter "alive" into death, that is to say, to live a full life before dying. I would like it said of me one day: "Ramón neither feared to die, nor refused to live."

Suffering: A Common Experience

To be human implies being confronted with painful situations. In fact, the process of development itself is already a source of suffering. To abandon the tranquility of infancy and early childhood in order to grow up into greater maturity is painful. There is also pain in the choices adolescents must make in their becoming adults. During adulthood, too, one must face painful challenges. This is also true for late adulthood when people are not always able to deal with physical and, oftentimes, economic difficulties. Finally, to confront our own dying experience, and death itself, independently of our own religious beliefs, can be a source of great suffering and despair for many people.

Nevertheless, there is another suffering that is more tragic than the ones involved in our own development, namely, the suffering that we inflict on others that is generated by our own behavior—even though the suffering inflicted on others is not always willful.

Dealing with the suffering generated by our own growing up process can be relatively easy. However, it is not always easy to integrate the suffering resulting from someone else's behavior against us. This is a question with which I have more difficulty, for which I have no easy answer: Why is it that some people who have been deeply wounded seem able to heal and to become empowered by their suffering while others, perhaps even less wounded, are very disturbed? At times, I hear people say "God has been with her or him." This seems to be an acknowledgment of God's presence in one's life in order to explain her or his resilience in suffering. Nonetheless, I believe that God is present in everyone's life.

There is not doubt that I have been wounded during my childhood but yet have been able to integrate my painful experiences and as a result consider myself more mature and more empowered than I once was. The first step in my healing process consisted in gaining the courage and capacity to name my own suffering, to identify it and eventually share it with significant others in my life. We know how one of the unwritten rules of "dysfunctional families" is to silence the painful and often abusive situations. Consequently, if someone risks speaking about these, he or she usually feels "guilty" for having broken the implicit law of silence. For this reason, one must overcome the silence that impairs the healing process.

Besides the difficult familial situations I have described in the introduction to this chapter, two other events have been a source of pain to me since my childhood. I have been obliged to face them in order to become a more mature adult. First, when I was about six years of age, I was sexually abused by someone known by my family. I was helping him paint the facade of the old family home and he took advantage, as often happens, of my innocence. I believe that my unconscious protected me quite well during my childhood and adolescence in the face of this painful experience. In fact, I remembered it only occasionally during these periods of my early life. However, when I did occasionally recall this experience, I always felt guilty, thinking that *I* did something dirty and bad. Nevertheless, during my adulthood I had to confront this abuse in a different way. It was then that I began to replace my guilt with my shame. Thus, not only had I to revive the suffering engendered by the abuse, but also to confront the bias of our society against adults who were abused during childhood.

Our Western society has developed a great concern for all kinds of abuse, especially the physical and sexual abuse of children, adolescents and women. However, once the abused children become adults, society considers them as "potential" abusers. This is a stigma that adds additional pain and suffering to those people who have already had to deal with a great amount of pain in their lives. Perhaps, it is for this reason that many adults, who have suffered some kind of abuse during childhood or adolescence, refuse to speak about it, in order to avoid becoming stigmatized. This additional painful situation, which is also a source of shame, impairs the healing process. It is for this reason that I have decided to speak about it, simply because abused people are not responsible for the abuse. Neither do they automatically become abusers.

The second painful experience that has accompanied my growing up process is depression. I now know quite well what it means when we speak about "child depression." Externally, I have always been an "easy-going" person. At High School I was a bright student with whom others liked to work and associate. I was a leader, and concerned for the well-being of others. Yet, inside myself I was often-times sad and afraid. It is not difficult to understand why this stems from the type of family situation that I have described above. In one way or another, I became a kind of "scapegoat" for my family. I was treated badly, as if I were a bad boy. I was threatened, frequently, with the fact that my family was considering putting me into a correctional institution as a discipline. This generated a lot of fear in me. However, I was not a bad boy, but someone who liked to be with others, who had a great imagination and who was transparent with my family about my innermost thoughts and actions. I have never had a hidden agenda in my life.

Depression caused me to live my life feeling a kind of emptiness that did not appear externally; it was a kind of "personal secret." I have been successful in my studies, and in my relationships, but internally I was living as if nothing really fulfilled me deeply.

The tendency to depression often accompanied me in my adult life, specially when I got tired. In a particular way, when for a while I lived alone, this depressive mood engendered in me some suicidal ideation. I remember a particular day in which I became very afraid for my own life. This experience was very painful to me. Knowing already the shame and stigma attached to suicide and to suicide-related events, I felt very disturbed by my own feelings. I realized immediately that I needed the help of my friends in order to deal with these suicidal thoughts. However, this has also been a situation obliging me to take some options, and to do something for myself. I recognized how my life was a precious gift to me that I must not destroy. Progressively, I was able to integrate the painful experiences of my life, and in so doing I have been learning a lot about them. I would not have become the person who I am today without them. My own suffering has transformed me. Two things have helped me in this transformation.

First, I must recognize the importance that imagination has played in my life. Imagination is not a way of evading the painful experiences of life, that is to say, of reality. Through our imagination we can transform those experiences and place our pain in a larger perspective. What is still more important, imagination is a source of hope, and is intrinsically related to it. Without imagination, there would be no hope. I have been a man of hope. Hope deeply defines my very being. Beyond all the difficulties that I have found in my life, I have never given up hope for something better or for a more wonderful life.

The second thing that has always helped me overcome the painful experiences of my life is the compassion I receive from others, particularly from significant others in my life and always from the love of God. Since my childhood faith in God has been an essential dimension of my life.

A Parable of Human and Divine Compassion

The Florentine poet Dante Alighieri (1265–1321) wrote *The Divine Comedy*, one of the masterpieces of world literature. Dante's book is divided into three parts: Hell, Purgatory and Paradise. His book is one of the most important, and influential descriptions of Christian popular belief in "life beyond death" as typical of the late Middle Ages. In fact, *The Divine Comedy* has continued to influence the belief of many of our contemporary Christians regarding the final destination after death.

Nevertheless, I have discovered another important story within this wonderful work which has become for me a hermeneutical tool for the understanding of human and divine compassion. Dante fell in love with Beatrice, a woman that he saw at some point in his life, with whom he probably never spoke, but who became to him a kind of "Muse." Beatrice died and went to Paradise. The whole story of *The Divine Comedy* describes Dante's itinerary through Hell and Purgatory until his arrival in Paradise where he might at last meet Beatrice. Nonetheless, to prevent Dante from being lost in the mist of so much pain suffered by those damned forever in Hell, or from the pain of being purified for minor sins in Purgatory, Beatrice sent him a guide, who became also a kind of help and mentor during Dante's itinerary through Hell and Purgatory. This guide was the Latin poet Virgil (70–19 B.C.), whom Dante admired.

The symbolic figure of Virgil in *The Divine Comedy* has enabled me to develop a narrative about human and divine compassion, that is to say, about the importance of other people and of God, in our lives, especially when we are visited by suffering. The company of Virgil helped Dante cope during his journey through Hell and Purgatory. Virgil does not prevent Dante from suffering in the presence of other people's pain, but Dante is not alone. In this sense, the role of Virgil in *The Divine Comedy* became for me a parable as to what human compassion really is. Other people cannot prevent our pain and suffering, but their compassionate presence can accompany us, even when they are silent, and support us on our way toward Paradise, the light at the end of our dark nights. Virgil's presence in Dante' life, as described in *The Divine Comedy*, is also a parable on Divine compassion. Its helps us understand the way in which God behaves with us when we are visited by suffering. God, as a Divine "Virgil," is with us, holding our hand and accompanying us, especially in the most difficult times.

For Christians, the compassion of God is described in a wonderful way by the Gospel of Luke, in the story of the *Prodigal Son* (15:11–32). This is to me a parable about *forgiveness* and *healing*. The story is well-known. A father had two sons, and the younger asked him to have the share of the property he would inherit eventually. The father agreed. I assume that the father, despite his own suffering at his son's decision to leave home, understood this younger son's need to have his own life experience. Probably, the father was a man of experience who had already lived a full life and knew within himself what life was about. Thus, his younger son went away and lived his own life by himself, until he came upon difficult times.

For the first time, not so long ago, I discovered something important in this parable: there is no dialogue between the father and the younger son. There is one with the older son, but no conversation with the younger. When this younger son asked for his part of the inheritance, the father accepted without saying anything at all. After that, when the prodigal son was in the process of his own conversion, namely, in his healing process, and finally came into the presence of his father he said, "Father, I have sinned against heaven and before you; I am no longer worthy to be called your son." (v. 21) The father did not reply to his son. The attitude of the father was simply to say to his slaves: "Quickly, bring out a robe – the best one – and put it on him; put a ring on his finger and sandals on his feet. And get the fatted calf and kill it, and let us eat and celebrate; for this son of mine was dead and is alive again; he was lost and is found!" So they celebrated. (vs. 22–24)

The lack of dialogue between the father and his younger son has a lot of *psychological* and *spiritual* implications. First, from a psychological point of view, we know how today, in the process of healing and reconciliation among people, it is essential to be able to say to someone: "You have hurt me." And to hear the one inflicting the injury say: "Yes, I am sorry. I know that I have wounded you." In the parable, the father did not need to say to his younger son: "My son, if you only knew how much I have suffered by your absence! How many times I went out searching for you, how much I have been waiting and longing for you. How many nights I have spent without being able to sleep thinking of you. How many times, unseen, I have cried because of your absence." This attitude of the father's silence on these issues actually liberated the younger son from his own guilt and shame. Probably, the father understood the pain of this younger son and wanted to avoid hurting him further.

Second, from a spiritual or religious perspective the silence of the father is also essential. The father did not say: "Yes, my son, you have sinned against heaven and before me. However, because I am a good father, I am able to receive you. Nevertheless, you must become worthy of again becoming a son of mine. You must merit my love." Nor did the father say: "Yes, my son, you have sinned against heaven and before me. Now, you must do penance and pay for your sins and mistakes."

The father, who gave life to his son in a free way, receives him in a free way, without adding any condition. This is how God behaves with us. This is how I have experienced divine compassion and the compassion of others. I recognized that compassion in those "Virgils" who have received me as I was, and when I needed them. I have been a *resilient* child. The fact of having been able to integrate the painful experiences of my life into a healthy maturity has been due to the "Virgils" I have found in the course of my life. They are the ones who took me by the hand and helped me pass through my own Hell and Purgatory.

The first "Virgil" in my life I met as a child. It was my paternal grandmother. She was married to my grandfather, a Spanish nobleman, a count who was also her uncle. They grew up in affluence, but because of adverse business circumstances, followed by the political situation previous to the Spanish Civil War (1936–1939), my grandparents lost their fortune. Feeling ashamed because of their misfortune, they moved to the South so as to avoid being embarrassed by their poverty. Perhaps for this reason I may have shame buried somewhere in my own genes.

However, my grandmother lived in poverty with the same dignity that she lived amid abundance. She was a talented and sensitive person and also a very religious one. She has probably been the one who has had the most influence in my entire life. I used to visit her almost daily. Her presence was to me like an "oasis" of peace and wisdom. She was to me like the wise women who teach us the mysteries of life simple by their presence. One day she almost died when we were alone. Again her peace and wisdom on that occasion seemed to be her last gift to me. Her love to me helped me to imagine and hope for something different in my own life. She allowed me to discover the greatest side of life. She was a very compassionate person to me and through her love for me I began to learn the importance of human compassion in the healing process.

I found the second "Virgil" of my life during my early adolescence. He was, and still is, a Roman Catholic priest and a member of the religious congregation to which I would eventually belong. When I met him, I was a High School student and very engaged in my Christian community. At that time I did not have any idea that one day I too would become a priest. I was thinking rather of becoming a medical doctor.

This priest helped me discover a compassionate God. As I have indicated, my paternal grandmother was a very religious person. Her spirituality was deep and sincere. I have in fact inherited my own faith from her. Nevertheless, I encountered a different God in my adolescence through this second "Virgil." Through him, I learned to recognize my own beauty and goodness in the face of God. This experience has also shaped my life deeply. To recognize that I deserved to be loved simply because I was a person. That I did not need to feel ashamed for things that had happened to me and for which I was not responsible. The discovery was that I was called to live a full life and to be happy, rather than thinking that it was God's will that I should suffer.

Contrary to the image of a punitive God that was often presented to me during the Sunday Religious School of my childhood and the sermons I heard in my adolescence, a God who was forever keeping a record of my own bad deeds, this priest helped me encounter a compassionate God who accompanies me in my life and who "takes me by the hand," particularly during my difficult experiences. This compassion of God has also been an important element in my healing process.

The third "Virgil" in my life I discovered when I was already in adulthood. He was a colleague of mine at the University. A psychologist and also a Roman Catholic priest, a member of my own religious congregation. He also has become one of my friends. He has been an excellent therapist to me, always open to receive me when I needed help.

This therapist helped me to discover and to integrate into my life the importance of my own "shadow," to use a Jungian term, or the dark side of my personality. This has helped me become a more integrated being. I feel now more empowered, in part because I have been able to learn to listen to this dark side of myself, rather than to deny and repress it. This helped me to realize that to be human means to be contingent and fragile, and thus to renounce the unhealthy desire to be perfect in everything. Integrating my "shadow" made me feel more whole, and also more realistic about myself.

More recently, I discovered a fourth "Virgil" in my life, in the form of a woman who died young a few years ago. However, she had lived a full life and was able to enter "alive" into her death.

She was physically limited because of several brain tumors progressively impairing her. Yet, I never saw her complain about her health. She was always thinking about how to help others. In many ways, she reminded me of my paternal grandmother. The secret of my friend's life, of her peace and wisdom, was her faith in God. In this regard, she became the most spiritual being I have ever met. Her life was for me what seemed like a divine gift, transforming me simply through her presence and, at the end of her life, when she was unable to speak anymore, through her silence. She was always full of life, with a desire to live each moment with intensity. She has helped me relativize my own suffering and to put it into a larger perspective. She has been to me a living incarnation of love that is both human and divine.

Finally, "Virgils" have also been to me those people who helped me to be in touch with my own limitations. Oftentimes, these have been people who have experienced the consequences of my mistakes, that is to say, those who have been wounded by me and have told me so.

To recognize that I also have the capacity to hurt others has been a little more difficult. However, this is one of the most important dimensions in my healing process. For it has allowed me to avoid the temptation to victimize myself. Furthermore, these various "Virgils" have helped me realize that no one else fully fills the emptiness in one's life. Only I myself, with the help of others, can do this. In this regard, these "Virgils" helped me revise my own expectations and enabled me to set up more realistic standards in my life. I am becoming now more empowered because I am seeing myself in a more integrated way in my healing process, accepting my own limits and mistakes.

I have just presented the "Virgils" that have helped me enter alive into death, namely, the ability to live my life fully in the face of the fact that I will surely die. In this sense, I am overcoming the shame that has poisoned my life over many years and especially in those few times that it prompted suicidal thoughts.

To Enter "Alive" into Death

I come from the city of Jaén that is also the capital of the most well-known Province in the world noted for the production of olive oil. I grew up surrounded by olive trees and mountains. I am very rooted in nature. The beauties of my native geographical landscapes shaped my life.

I developed an attraction for flowers, particularly roses. Roses helped me discover one of the most important dimensions of life: to live fully before dying. When we put a bouquet of roses in a vase with water, in just a few hours the roses begin to open, to reveal all their beauty. That is a wonderful experience. There are no two roses that are the same. Each one has a different tonality in its color. Not only this, but also if we observe the petals, there are no two petals alike. Each one has a different shape. With practice it is possible to feel their difference by touching them. There is no rivalry in beauty, only harmonic complementarity. Nonetheless, for some strange reason, it sometimes does happen that a rosebuds fails to open and ends up wilted, never having revealed its splendour. This is unfortunate, for its real beauty will forever remain hidden.

Life is to me like a bouquet of roses that each of us embodies as a gift, in order to blossom fully. No two lives are the same. Each has a particular quality that others do not have. For this reason, too, there can be no real rivalry between our respective talents and beauty, only complementarity. Nevertheless, it sometimes happens, as with a bouquet of roses, that some people die without having been able to blossom and live life to the full. They bring their unsung beauty and talents to the grave with them.

My work in residences for the sick and elderly has taught me to recognize that it is the totality of human experience that enables a person either to enter alive into death or to see dying and death as the greatest misfortune. It is a tragic experience to face the mess one has made of one's life; and it is a tragedy not have truly lived. Too often people come to the end of their existence feeling wilted and realizing they have not fulfilled their purpose. That is a failed life, one that is closed in upon itself. Thus, I think that some cemeteries represent not so much death as lives with talents that have been buried forever. Here there may repose the remains of people who have not truly lived. At the end of their lives, many come to realize that they have failed and, in consequence, would like to have another chance. This is one of the reasons for the present attraction to reincarnation in Western society, which promotes the notion that death is simply one temporary passage among several to come, thus denying the true mysterious side of death and of life.

To die before having lived a full life makes us feel sad. I believe that beyond any shame and stigmatization attached to suicide one of the things that makes us feel bad in the face of this tragedy is the realization that some people die before having fully lived their own lives. This is particularly true regarding the suicide of adolescents. As we have already note in the Introduction to this book, the adolescent population is one that has the highest rate of suicide.

However, in order to enter "alive" into death one must recognize and integrate the painful experiences of life. In this regard, the beginning of my own healing process took place around the year 1988. I went to visit my family doctor for the results of some previous medical tests. It was then that my doctor told me: "Ramón, you have an ulcer." To me, this was a shock. I already knew the importance of psychosomatic mechanisms. I knew how an ulcer was also the result of my own way of being and living. When I shared this bad news with my friends, they too became surprised. I always appeared like a happy go-lucky person. In the beginning it was difficult to integrate this experience positively in my life.

To add to this difficulty, it all coincided with a depression I had after finishing my doctorate in Theology, at a time when I fell in love with a woman. To be in love, for the first time as an adult, was a truly wonderful even if painful experience in my life. I had to stop intellectualizing it and accept it as a reality of life.

How could a Roman Catholic priest possibly fall in love? It was then that I had to accept and deal with the reality of my being human. This was an experience that has transformed me deeply. In the end I had to make some painful decisions in order to continue journeying on the path I had chosen in my life.

I decided that I was not going to jeopardize my healing process. I went to speak with my friend, the therapist. Then I initiated my own way of healing. In this process, memory played an essential role. I have already spoken about the role that imagination played in my life. Now, I need to say something about the importance of remembering. Remembering the painful experiences of our lives is a key dimension in the healing process.

For this reason, I do not agree with the lyrics of French singer Charles Aznavour, who, in one of his songs, sings: "I believe that memory is the enemy of our dreams." Memory is not the enemy of our dreams, but the way through which we can heal the painful experiences of our life. Remembering them helps us avoid their repetition. This is essential in the therapeutic process. Naming the painful events of our life is the beginning of our healing process. Consequently, I can well appreciate the expression written in some of the concentration camps in Europe after the liberation from the Nazi holocaust during World War II: "Forgive, but do not forget."

To confront my ulcer, the depression following my doctorate in theology, and the fact of suddenly falling in love, allowed me to initiate the process of remembering the experiences I have described above. This process has transformed my life for ever. I am no longer the fearful and ashamed child and adolescent that I once was. My healing process has empowered me. I now consider myself like a precious piece of marble, a person that is being sculptured and shaped into life, and thus a person fully alive to life.

Conclusion

I spoke of imagination and its important role in my healing process. On several occasions, I imagined what I would do if I were God.

In Christian tradition, as well as in some other religious traditions, it is believed that, after our death, we will come into the presence of God. It is then that God will determine whether or not we deserve to live forever in Paradise. Thus, if I were God, I would ask everyone to write an essay before he or she were allowed to enter Heaven. However, I would not ask them to write about their personal misdeeds, faults or limitations. The "sins" that we all commit in life are, after all, pretty much the same ones for everyone. There is no originality in defining or listing our moral shortcomings. I would rather ask them to write about those talents and gifts which they had received in life but, for various and sundry reasons, were not able to make blossom fully in this world.

Paradise, heaven, is life everlasting. As I have indicated above, one has to enter "alive" into death. Therefore, such an essay might help people become reconciled with all the wonderful gifts they have had in their lives yet may not have been able to explore as a way to becoming fully alive in eternal life.

I have spoken here about my own efforts to overcome the painful experiences of my life but it was not only a personal and private quest. I have to say that I also consider my healing process to be more than the result of my own determination but also a Divine gift. For this reason, it now becomes possible for me to open my hands and let things go; to be able to forgive those who have hurt me in my life, particularly when I was a child and a young adolescent; and this implies my having the courage and honesty to recognize that I need the forgiveness of others as well. The forgiveness of those wounded by my own limits.

I have a friend who used to say to me: "Ramón, life is too short." Yes, indeed, she was right, "life is too short." For this reason, each moment is "eternity." Quite often in my life, I lived in the future, imagining a better situation, or in the past, remembering painful experiences. I lost a lot of "present moments" when I was a child and an adolescent. I grew old too soon in my life and I have the impression that my early life was lived by someone else. Therefore, to become empowered by healing has helped me live my present life, each precious moment at a time, as the single most important gifts I have received.

Finally, in order to live a full life, I had to recognize the importance of becoming a more transparent person. This is what obliged me to name and to confront my painful experiences. This is the process I undertook to become a more empowered self through healing.

Summary and General Conclusions

Suicide is one of the leading causes of violent death in Western society. On May 21, 2003, Zenit International News Agency [Z.I.N.A.], in its electronic Daily Dispatch/News Briefs, reported on a congress on "Suicide: Option, Madness, or Mystery?" which was held that month at the "Camillianum" International Institute of Pastoral and Health Theology in Rome. According to the report, there is "an increase in the suicide rate of adolescents in countries with a high standard of living such as Germany, Denmark, Finland, Austria, and Switzerland,"[1] and I would add, doubtless, in North America. In the same news item it was reported that "About 5,000 people commit suicide every day."[2] As I have underlined in the Introduction to this book, statistics on suicide do not reflect the full reality. The real number of suicides is even higher.

In fact, we already know that adolescents and the elderly are the two populations at highest risk for committing or attempting suicide. This situation reflects certain destructive aspects of the North American way of life to which people are increasingly turning their attention. These can be considered as "ideologies," rather than as an expression of real cultural values, the latter being, according to Richard G. Cote, always good and positive dimensions of a society. There is no doubt that today one of the most important things for many people is *power* in its different manifestations: money, fame, youth, and so forth. The "ideology" of power is not synonymous with the "core" American cultural value which enjoins one to be "FREE, STRONG, ENTERPRISING, and INNOVATIVE."[3]

An example of the "ideology" of power is what happens in the educational system. One of the words which can be frequently heard in an educational milieu is "excellence," which is almost invariably equated with *intellectual performance.* But human beings are not merely performers, intellectually or otherwise. They are also called to integrate other dimensions of life and of their humanity such as giftedness, friendship, love, generosity, and so on. To try to perform at any cost is, as was underlined in the second chapter, something that can lead perfectionists, in particular, talented students, to commit or to attempt suicide in order to avoid the feelings of failure and shame at their own continued inability to succeed at an unrealistic level in an unrealistic endeavor. To confuse excellence with intellectual performance has some negative implications.[4] This confusion may explain why some educational systems are real failures. Often they generate "monsters," people with great intelligence who are otherwise unable to confront existential challenges such as pain, illness, death, dying and the process of bereavement. Frequently, these persons arrive at the end of their life cycle without having developed their talents fully. In other words, many feel that their lives are a failure, and failure, as we can remember, is at the source of shame. Suicide can then be considered as a way of dealing with this painful situation. The emphasis on *power* at whatever cost impairs the capacity, particularly among adolescents and the elderly, to confront the painful experiences of life in a healthy manner.

Arnaldo Pangrazzi, the deputy director of the "Camillianum" Institute, spoke in an address on suicide of how "in rich countries people who attempt to commit suicide feel the contrast between external beauty and peace and their interior world lacerated by profound conflicts."[5] This extreme contrast reveals some of the most important reasons for committing or attempting suicide: alienation from oneself and from others and hopelessness regarding the future, too often resulting in depression and alcoholism, or other substance abuse.

In my fourth chapter, I referred to one of the main topics mentioned by Robert I. Yufit in his presidential address to the annual meeting of the American Association of Suicidology on April 26, 1990, namely, the need to help people, particularly the young, but also adults and the elderly, to cope better with the stressful experiences of life.[6] Lack of problem-solving and communication skills impairs the capacity of dealing with those difficult events, even vitiating the perception of reality. In this sense, the incapacity to share problems with significant others can become another trigger for suicide or a suicide attempt that needs to be taken seriously in order to avoid its lethal consequences. Therefore, educational programs at all levels are needed to help people develop healthy skills in order to deal with stressful experiences. Furthermore, school prevention programs for detecting those at high risk of suicide, and for coping with the bereavement process of student survivors of the suicide of an acquaintance, are also necessary.

Even though we know that suicide is a complex reality whose causes we cannot pretend to have exhausted, I have sought, following the theory of Lazarus and Folkman on coping with stress, to present shame as a personal and environmental constraint that impedes the ability to cope in a healthy way with suicide and attempted suicides. In itself, chronic shame sometimes spoils one's capacity to mature, resulting in suicide, the final, most extreme result of excessive shame. Suicide also fosters undue shame in survivors and in those who have attempted suicide without succeeding. Finally, the relationship between shame and suicide is also mediated by the stigma attached to suicide, even if shame itself is at the origin of the stigmatization of suicide before becoming its result. Thus, taking into consideration the important negative link between shame and suicide, further research into this particular relationship is needed to better understand this maladaptive connection and to defeat its lethal results.

This book has been written with the personal wish to help people wounded by shame and suicide to overcome their negative and often pathological consequences. I have found that the most important dimension in the process of healing dysfunctional shame, in its special link with suicide and suicide-related events, is to be able to recognize it, to accept it, and to share with significant others the painful experiences triggered by toxic shame as a cause or consequence of suicide. Fragility and vulnerabilities are essential dimensions of being human, and not necessarily manifestations of weaknesses or imperfections. In order to overcome the negative consequences of the relationship between shame and suicide, a transformation of socio-cultural and religious attitudes toward suicide is needed. Only then shall we be able to look at suicide without denying its reality and to confront its negative consequences.

This research does not claim to deal with all the dimensions of suicide. Rather, it emphasized the particular link between chronic shame and suicide. What is more, I have tried to portray this deadly relationship in a way that is understandable to most readers. I myself have sometimes had difficulties in working through the amount of empirical research on shame and on suicide. Reading such material can often leave one indifferent because of one's lack of technical formation in the area of statistics. For this reason, I have tried to present in this book what I have considered to be the substance of this research so that others may more fully understand and recognize the tragic reality of suicide and its particular link to chronic shame in a more existential and comprehensive way .

In the Judeo-Christian tradition, life is seen as a wonderful Divine gift that humans and other creatures receive freely. Human life is not intended to be a "Valley of Tears," and we are not obliged to live forever with the burden of shame as a cause or consequence of suicide. We are called instead to overcome its negativism in order to become more mature in a fulfilling and responsible life, one in which we are able to share our life with others in a healthy way.

Notes

[1]   Z.I.N.A., 2003.
[2]   Z.I.N.A., 2003.
[3]   Cote, 1996, p. 135. Upper case in the original text.
[4]   Feshbach et al., 1996.
[5]   Z.I.N.A., 2003.
[6]   Yufit, 1991.

Bibliography

Aldwin, C. M. (1994). *Stress, coping, and development: An integrative perspective.* New York, NY/London, UK: The Guilford Press.

Alexander, V. (1991). Grief after suicide: Giving voice to the loss. *Journal of Geriatric Psychiatry, 24,* 277–291.

Allen, B. G., Calhoun, L. G., Cann, A., & Tedeschi, R. D. (1993–94). The effect of cause of death on responses to the bereaved: Suicide compared to accident and natural causes. *Omega: Journal of Death and Dying, 28, 1,* 39–48.

Apter, A., Horesh, N., Gothelf, D., Graffi, H., & Lepkifker, E. (2001). Relationship between self-disclosure and serious suicidal behavior. *Comprehensive Psychiatry, 42, 1,* 70–75.

Ariès, P. (1967). La mort inversée: Le changement des attitudes devant la mort dans les sociétés occidentales. *Archives Européenes de Sociologie, VIII,* 169–195.

Ariès, P. (1974). *Western attitudes toward death: From the Middle Ages to the present* (P. M. Ranum, Trans.). Baltimore, MD/London, UK: The Johns Hopkins University Press.

Ayyash-Abdo, H. (2002). Adolescent suicide: An ecological approach. *Psychology in the Schools, 39, 4,* 459–475.

Bailley, S. E., Kral, M. J., & Dunham, K. (1999). Survivors of suicide do grieve differently: Empirical support for a common sense proposition. *Suicide and Life-Threatening Behavior, 29, 3,* 256–271.

Barber, J. G. (2001). Relative misery and youth suicide. *Australian & New Zealand Journal of Psychiatry, 35, 1,* 49–57.

Barrett, T. W., & Scott, T. B. (1989). Development of the Grief Experience Questionnaire. *Suicide and Life-Threatening Behavior, 19, 2,* 201–215.

Barrios, L. C., Everett, S. A., Simon, T. R., & Brener, N. D. (2000). Suicide ideation among US college students: Associations with other injury risk behaviors. *Journal of American College Health, 48, 5,* 229–233.

Baumeister, R. F. (1990). Suicide as escape from self. *Psychological Review, 97, 1,* 90–113.

Beautrais, A. L. (2000). Risk factors for suicide and attempted suicide among young people. *Australian and New Zealand Journal of Psychiatry, 34, 3,* 420–436.

Beck, A. T. (1967). *Depression: Clinical, experimental, and theoretical aspects.* New York, NY: Hoeber Medical Division, Harper & Row, Publishers, Incorporated.

Beck, A. T., Kovacs, M., & Weissman, A. (1975). Hopelessness and suicidal behavior: An overview. *JAMA: The Journal of the American Medical Association, 234, 11,* 1146–1149.

Bensley, L. S., Van Eenwyk, J., Spieker, S. J., & Schoder, J. (1999). Self-reported abuse history and adolescent problem behaviors: I. Antisocial and suicidal behaviors. *Journal of Adolescent Health, 24, 3,* 163–172.

Bifulco, A., Moran, P. M., Baines, R., Bunn, A., & Standord, K. (2002). Exploring psychological abuse in childhood: II. Association with other abuse and adult clinical depression. *Bulletin of the Menninger Clinic, 66, 3,* 241–258.

Black, D. W., Yates, W., Petty, F., Noyes, R., & Brown, K. (1986). Suicidal behavior in alcoholic males. *Comprehensive Psychiatry, 27,* 227–233.

Bradshaw, J. (1988). *Healing the shame that binds you.* Deerfield Beach, FL: Health Communications, Inc.

Breed, W. (1972). Five component of basic suicide syndrome. *Life-Threatening Behavior 2, 1,* 3–18.

Bregman, L. (1999). *Beyond silence and denial: Death and dying reconsidered.* Louisville, KY: Westminster John Knox Press.

Calhoun, L. G., & Allen, B. G. (1991). Social reactions to the survivor of a suicide in the family: A review of the literature. *Omega: Journal of Death and Dying, 23, 2,* 95–107.

Catechism of the Catholic Church [C.C.C.]. (1993). Ottawa, ON: Canadian Conference of Catholic Bishops.

Chance, S. (1992). *Stronger than death.* New York, NY/London, UK: W. W. Norton & Company, Inc.

Christ, A. E. (1961). Attitudes toward death among a group of acute geriatric psychiatric patients. *Journal of Gerontology, 16,* 56–59.

Clark, S. E., & Goldney, R. D. (1995). Grief reactions and recovery in a support group for people bereaved by suicide. *Crisis: The Journal of Crisis Intervention and Suicide Prevention, 16, 1,* 27–33.

Clark, S. E., Jones, H. E., Quinn, K., Goldney, R. D., & Cooling, P. J. (1993). A support group for people bereaved through suicide. *Crisis: The Journal of Crisis Intervention and Suicide Prevention, 14, 4,* 161–167.

Clayton, P. I. (1993). Suicide in panic disorder and depression. *Current Therapeutic Research, 54, 6,* 825–831.

Clemons, J. T. (1990). *What the Bible say about suicide?* Minneapolis, MN: Fortress Press.

Codex iuris canonici. (1917). Romae: Typis Polyglottis Vaticanis.

Conner, K. R., Duberstein, P. R., Conwell, Y., Seidlitz, L., & Caine, E. D. (2001). Psychological vulnerability to completed suicide: A review of empirical studies. *Suicide & Life-Threatening Behavior, 31, 4,* 367–385.

Conwell, Y., Dubertstein, P. R., & Caine, E. D. (2002). Risk factors for suicide in later life. *Biological Psychiatry, 52, 3,* 193–204.

Corens, S., & Hewitt, P. L. (1999). Sex differences in elderly suicide rates: Some predictive factors. *Aging & Mental Health, 3, 2,* 112–118.

Cote, R. G. (1996). *Re-visioning mission: The Catholic Church and culture in postmodern America.* New York, NY/Mahwah, NJ: Paulist Press.

DiFilippo, J. M., & Overholser, J. C. (2000). Suicidal ideation in adolescent psychiatric inpatients as associated with depression and attachment relationships. *Journal of Clinical Child Psychology, 29, 2,* 155–166.

"Dignity at the end of life." (2004). *Journal of Palliative Care, 20, 3,* a whole thematic issue.

Doe, N. (1998). *Canon law in the Anglican Communion: A worldwide perspective.* Oxford, UK: Oxford University Press.

Dunn, R. G., & Morrish-Vidners, D. (1987–88). The psychological and social experience of suicide survivors. *Omega: Journal of Death and Dying, 18, 3,* 175–215.

Ellens, J. H. (1982). *God's Grace and Human Health.* Nashville, TN: Abingdon.

Ellens, J. H. (Ed.). (2004). *The destructive power of religion: Violence in Judaism, Christianity, and Islam (vols. I–IV).* Westport, CT: Praeger.

Exline, J. J., Yali, A. M., & Sanderson, W. C. (2000). Guilt, discord, and alienation: The role of religious strain in depression and suicidality. *Journal of Clinical Psychology, 56, 12,* 1481–1496.

Farberow, N. L., Gallagher-Thompson, D. E., Gilewski, M. J., & Thompson, L. W. (1992a). Changes in grief and mental health of bereaved spouses of older suicides. *Journal of Gerontology, 47, 6,* 357–366.

Farberow, N. L., Gallagher-Thompson, D. E., Gilewski, M. J., & Thompson, L. W. (1992b). The role of social supports in the bereavement process of surviving spouses of suicide and natural deaths. *Suicide and Life-Threatening Behavior, 22, 1,* 107–124.

Fasullo, S., & Guarneri, M. (1993). Malinconia e suicidio: L'oralità bramosa. *Giornaly Italiano di Suicidologia, 3, 2,* 117–120.

Feshbach, S., Weiner, B., & Bohart, A. (1996). *Personality* (4th ed.). Lexington, MA: D. C. Health and Company.

Fossum, M. A., & Mason, M. J. (1986). *Facing shame: Families in recovery.* New York, NY/London, UK: W. W. Norton & Company, Inc.

Fox, R., & Cooper, M. (1998). The effects of suicide on the private practitioner: A professional and personal perspective. *Clinical Social Work Journal, 26, 2,* 143–157.

Fritsch, S., Donaldson, D., Spirito, A., & Plummer, B. (2000). Personality characteristics of adolescent suicide attempters. *Child Psychiatry and Human Development, 30, 4,* 219–235.

Frølund, L. (1997). Early shame and mirroring. *The Scandinavian Psychoanalytic Review, 20, 1,* 35–57.

Furr, S. R., McConnel, G. N., Westefeld, J. S., & Jenkins, J. M. (2001). Suicide and depression among college students: A decade later. *Professional Psychology: Research and Practice, 32, 1,* 97–100.

Gaulejac, V. de (1996). *Les sources de la honte.* Paris: Desclée de Brouwer.

Glaser, B. G., & Strauss, A. L. (1980). *Awareness of dying* (Rev. ed.). New York, NY: Aldine Pub. Co.

Godney, R. D., Spence, N. D., & Moffitt, P. F. (1987). The aftermath of suicide: Attitudes of those bereaved by suicide, of social workers, and of a community sample. *Journal of Community Psychology, 15,* 141–148.

Goldberg, C. (1991). *Understanding shame.* Northvale, NJ/London, UK: Jason Aronson Inc.

Goldstein, S. (1989). *Suicide in the Rabbinic literature.* Hoboken, NJ: Ktav Publishing House, Inc.

Goldston, D. B., Daniel, S. S., Reboussin, B. A., Reboussin, D. M., Frazier, P. H., & Harris, A. E. (2001). Cognitive risk factors and suicide attempts among formerly hospitalized adolescents: A prospective naturalistic study. *Journal of the American Academy of Child & Adolescent Psychiatry, 40, 1,* 91–99.

Gormly, A. V., & Brodzinsky, D. M. (1993). *Lifespan human development* (5th ed.). Orlando, Fl: Harcourt Brace & Company.

Gould, M. S., Fisher, P., Parides, M., Flory, M., & Shaffer, D. (1996). Psychosocial risk factors of child and adolescent completed suicide. *Archives of General Psychiatry, 53, 12,* 1155–1162.

Grad, O. T., Zavasnik, A., & Groleger, U. (1997). Suicide of a patient: Gender differences in bereavement reactions of therapists. *Suicide and Life-Threatening Behavior, 27, 4,* 379–386.

Gramzow, R., & Tangney, J. P. (1992). Proneness to shame and the narcissistic personality. *Personality and Social Psychology Bulletin, 18, 3,* 369–376.

Gunnell, D. J. (2000). The epidemiology of suicide. *International Review of Psychiatry, 12, 1,* 21– 26.

Gust-Brey, K., & Cross, T. (1999). An examination of the literature base on the suicidal behaviors of gifted students. *Roeper Review, 22, 1,* 28–35.

Gutierrez, P. M., Osman, A., Kopper, B. A., Barrios, F. X., & Bagge, C. L. (2000). Suicide risk assessment in a college student population. *Journal of Counseling Psychology, 47, 4,* 403–413.

Gyulay, J. E. (1989). What suicide leaves behind. *Issues in Comprehensive Pediatric Nursing, 12,1,* 103–118.

Hahn, W. K. (2000). Shame: Countertransference identifications in individual psychotherapy. *Psychotherapy: Theory/Research/Practice/Training, 37, 1,* 10–21.

Halling, S. (1994). Shame and forgiveness. *The Humanistic Psychologist, 22, 1,* 74–87.

Hardt, D. V. (1979). *Death: The final frontier.* Englewood Cliffs, NJ: Prentice-Hall.

Harper, J. M., & Hoopes, M. H. (1990). *Uncovering shame: An approach integrating individuals and their family systems.* New York, NY/London, UK: W. W. Norton & Company, Inc.

Harry, T. E., & Lennings, C. J. (1993). Suicide and adolescence. *International Journal of Offender Therapy and Comparative Criminology, 37, 3,* 263–270.

Heikkinen, M., Aro, H., & Lönnqvist, J. (1993). Life events and social support in suicide. *Suicide and Life-Threatening Behavior, 23, 4,* 343–358.

Hibbard, S. (1992). Narcissism, shame, masochism, and object relations: An exploratory correlational study. *Psychoanalytic Psychology, 9, 4,* 489–508.

Hockenberry, S. L. (1995). Dyadic violence, shame, and narcissism. *Contemporary Psychoanalysis, 31, 2,* 301–325.

Holden, R. R., & Kroner, D. G. (2003). Differentiating suicidal motivations and manifestations in a forensic sample. *Canadian Journal of Behavioural Science/Revue canadienne des sciences du comportement, 35, 1,* 35–44.

Hoxey, K., & Shah, A. (2000). Recent trends in elderly suicide rates in England and Wales. *International Journal of Geriatric Psychiatry, 15, 3,* 274–279.

Hufford, M. R. (2001). Alcohol and suicidal behavior. *Clinical Psychology Review, 21, 5,* 797–811.

Ikonen, P., & Rechardt, E. (1993). The origin of shame and its vicissitudes. *Scandinavian Psychoanalytic Review, 16, 2,* 1000–1124.

Jacoby, M. (1994). *Shame and the origins of self-esteem: A Jungian approach* (D. Whitcher, & M. Jacoby, Trans.). London, UK/New York, NY: Routledge.

Jaques, J. D. (2000). Surviving suicide: The impact on the family. *The Family Journal: Counseling and Therapy for Couples and Families, 8, 4,* 376–379.

Jordan, J. R. (2001). Is suicide bereavement different? A reassessment of the literature. *Suicide and Life-Threatening Behavior, 31, 1,* 91–102.

Kalafat, J., & Lester, D. (2000). Shame and suicide: A case study. *Death Studies, 24, 2,* 157–162.

Kaplan, S. J., Pelcovitz, D., Salzinger, S., Mandel, F., Weiner, M., & Labruna, V. (1999). Adolescent physical abuse and risk for suicidal behaviors. *Journal of International Violence, 14, 9,* 976–988.

Kaufman, G. (1989). *The psychology of shame: Theory and treatment of shame-based syndromes.* New York, NY: Springer Publishing Company.

Klinger, J. (1999). Suicide among seniors. *Australasian Journal on Ageing, 18, 3,* 114–118.

Knieper, A. J. (1999). The suicide survivor's grief and recovery. *Suicide and Life-Threatening Behavior, 29, 4,* 353–364.

Kübler-Ross, E. (1975). *Death: The final stage of growth.* Englewood Cliffs, NJ: Prentice-Hall.

Kübler-Ross, E. (1978). *On death and dying.* New York, NY: Macmillan.

Kurtz, L., & Derevensky, J. L. (1993). Stress and coping in adolescents: The effects of family -configuration and environment on suicidality. *Canadian Journal of School Psychology, 9, 2,* 204–216.

Laderman, G. (2000). The Disney way of death. *Journal of the American Academy of Religion, 68, 1,* 27–46.

Lansky, M. R. (1991). Shame and the problem of suicide: A family systems perspective. *British Journal of Psychotherapy, 7, 3,* 230–242.

Lansky, M. R. (1996). Shame and suicide in Sophocles' *Ajax. Psychoanalytic Quarterly, LXV, 4,* 761–786.

Lazarus, R. S. (1966). *Psychological stress and the coping process.* New York, NY: McGraw-Hill Book Company.

Lazarus, R. S. (1999). *Stress and emotion: A new synthesis.* New York, NY: Springer Publishing Company, Inc.

Lazarus, R. S., & Folkman, S. (1984). *Stress, appraisal, and coping.* New York, NY: Springer Publishing Company, Inc.

Leenaars, A., & Connolly, J. (2001). Suicide, assisted suicide and euthanasia: International perspectives. *Irish Journal of Psychological Medicine, 18, 1,* 33–37.

Leonard, E. C. Jr. (2001). Confidential death to prevent suicidal contagion: An accepted, but never implemented, nineteenth-century idea. *Suicide & Life-Threatening Behavior, 31, 4,* 460–466.

Lester, D. (1997). The role of shame in suicide. *Suicide and Life-Threatening Behavior, 27, 4,* 352–361.

Lewis, H. B. (1971). *Shame and guilt in neurosis.* New York, NY: International Universities Press.

Lewis, H. B. (1987a). Introduction: Shame-the "sleeper" in psychopathology. In H. B. Lewis (Ed.), *The role of shame in symptom formation* (pp. 1–28). Hillsdale, NJ/London, UK: Lawrence Erlbaum Associates, Publishers.

Lewis, H. B. (1987b). The role of shame in depression over the life span. In H. B. Lewis (Ed.), *The role of shame in symptom formation* (pp. 29–50). Hillsdale, N.J./London, U.K.: Lawrence Erlbaum Associates, Publishers.

Lewis, M. (1992). *Shame: The exposed self.* New York, NY: The Free Press.

Lifton, R. J. (1980). *The broken connexion: On death and the continuity of life.* New York, NY: Basic Books.

Lombardi, D. N., Florentino, M. C., & Lombardi, A. J. (1998). Perfectionism and abnormal behavior. *The Journal of Individual Psychology, 54, 1,* 61–71.

Martínez de Pisón, R. (2002). Shame, death, and dying. *Pastoral Psychology, 51, 1,* 27–40.

Marttunen, M. J., Aro, H. M., & Lönnqvist, J. K. (1993). Precipitant stressors in adolescent suicide. *Journal of the American Academy of Child and Adolescent Psychiatry, 32, 6,* 1178–1183.

Marzouki, M. (1990). *La mort apprivoisée: Le médecin et la mort.* Montreal, QC: Méridien.

Mattox, R. J., & Peck, G. (1992). Shame or guilt: A perspective for therapists. *Psychology: A Journal of Human Behavior, 29, 2,* 18–25.

Mauk, G. W., & Weber, C. (1991). Peer survivors of adolescent suicide: Perspectives on grieving and postvention. *Journal of Adolescent Research, 6, 1,* 113–131.

Mayfield, D. G., & Montgomery, D. (1972). Alcoholism, alcohol intoxication, and suicide attempts. *Archives of General Psychiatry, 27,* 349–353.

McClelland, L., Reicher, S., & Booth, N. (2000). A last defense: The negotiation of blame within suicide notes. *Journal of Community & Applied Social Psychology, 10, 3,* 225–240.

McIntosh, J. L., & Kelly, L. D. (1992). Survivors' reactions: Suicide vs. other causes. *Crisis: The Journal of Crisis Intervention and Suicide Prevention, 13, 1,* 82–93.

McIntosh, J. L., & Wrobleski, A. (1988). Grief reactions among suicide survivors: An exploratory comparison of relationships. *Death Studies, 12,* 21–39.

Miles, J. (1997). *God: A biography.* New York, NY: Knopf.

Miles, J. (2001). *Christ: A crisis in the life of God,* New York, NY: Knopf.

Mokros, H. B. (1995). Suicide and shame. *American Behavioral Scientist, 38, 8,* 1091–1103.

Murphy, S. A., Johnson, L. C., Wu, L., Fan, J. J., & Lohan, J. (2003). Bereaved parents' outcomes 4 to 60 months after their children's death by accident, suicide, or homicide: A comparative study demonstrating differences. *Death Studies, 27, 1,* 39–61.

Murphy, S. A., Tapper, V. J., Johnson, L. C., & Lohan, J. (2003). Suicide ideation among parents bereaved by the violent deaths of their children. *Issues in Mental Health Nursing, 24, 1,* 5–25.

Nathanson, D. L. (1992). *Shame and pride: Affect, sex, and the birth of the self.* New York, NY/ London, UK: W. W. Norton & Company, Inc.

Nelson, B. J., & Frantz, T. T. (1996). Family interactions of suicide survivors and survivors of non-suicidal death. *Omega: Journal of Death and Dying, 33, 2,* 131–146.

Nouwen, H. J. M. (1975). *Reaching out: The three movements of the spiritual life.* Garden City, NY: Doubleday & Company, Inc.

Parkes, C. M. (1985). Bereavement. *British Journal of Psychiatry, 146,* 11–17.

Parsons, T. (1963). Death in American society: A brief working paper. *The American Behavioral Scientist, 6,* 61–65.

Pattison, S. (2000). *Shame: Theory, therapy, theology.* Cambridge, UK: Cambridge University Press.

Perrez, M., & Riecherts, M. (1992). *Stress, coping, and health: A situation-behavior approach: Theory, methods, applications.* Seattle/Toronto/Bern/Göttingen: Hogrefe & Huber Publishers.

Potter-Efron, P. S., & Potter-Efron, R. T. (1999). *The secret message of shame: Pathways to hope and healing.* Oakland, CA: New Harbinger Publications, Inc.

Pritchard, C., & Baldwin, D. S. (2002). Elderly suicide rates in Asian and English-speaking countries. *Acta Psychiatrica Scandinavica, 105, 4,* 271–275.

Provini, C., Everett, J. R., & Pfeffer, C. R. (2000). Adults mourning suicide: Self-reported concerns about bereavement, needs for assistance, and help-seeking behavior. *Death Studies, 24, 1,* 1–19.

Range, L. M., Leach, M. M., McIntyre, D., Posey-Deters, P. B., Marion, M. S., Kovac, S. H., Baños, J. H., & Vigil, J. (1999). Multicultural perspectives on suicide. *Aggression and Violent Behavior, 4, 4,* 413–430.

Reed, M. D. (1993). Sudden death and bereavement outcomes: The impact of resources on grief symptomatology and detachment. *Suicide and Life-Threatening Behavior, 23, 3,* 204–220.

Reed, M. D., & Greenwald, J. Y. (1991). Survivor-victim status, attachment, and sudden death bereavement. *Suicide and Life-Threatening Behavior, 21, 4,* 385–401.

Retzinger, S. M. (1989). A theory of mental illness: Integrating social and emotional aspects. *Psychiatry, 52,* 325–338.

Retzinger, S. M. (1991). *Violent emotions: Shame and rage in marital quarrels.* Newbury Park, CA: Sage.

Richards, B. M. (1999). Suicide and internalised relationships: A study from the perspective of psychotherapists working with suicidal patients. *British Journal of Guidance & Counseling, 27, 1,* 85–98.

Rizzuto, A. M. (1991). Shame in psychoanalysis: The function of unconscious fantasies. *International Journal of Psycho-Analysis, 72, 2,* 297–313.

Robertson, J. (1999). Dying to tell: Sexuality and suicide in Imperial Japan. *Signs: Journal of Women in Cultural and Society, 25, 1,* 1–35.

Roff, S. (2001). Suicide and the elderly: Issues for clinical practice. *Journal of Gerontological Social Work, 35, 2,* 21–36.

Rosenhan, D. L., & Seligman, M. E. P. (1995). *Abnormal psychology* (3rd ed.). New York, NY/London, UK: W. W. Norton & Company, Inc.

Rowe, D. (1991). Suicide and death. In C. Newnes (Ed.), *Death, dying and society* (pp. 262–269). Hove and London, UK/Hillsdale, PA: Lawrence Erlbaum Associates, Publishers.

Roy, A. (1993). Risk factors for suicide among adult alcoholics. *Alcohol, Health & Research World, 17, 2,* 133–136.

Roy, A. (2001). Brief reports. *The Journal of Nervous and Mental Disease, 189, 2,* 120–121.

Scheff, T. J. (1990). *Microsociology: Discourse, emotion and social structure.* Chicago, IL: University of Chicago Press.

Scheff, T. J. (1994). *Bloody revenge: Emotions, nationalism, and war.* Boulder, CO: Westview.

Scheff, T. J. (1997). *Emotions, the social bond, and human reality.* Cambridge, UK: Cambridge University Press.

Schmidtke, A., Weinacker, B., Apter, A., Batt, A., Berman, A., Bille-Brahe, U., Botsis, A., De Leo, D., Doneux, A., Goldney, R., Grad, O., Haring, C., Hawton, K., Hjelmeland, H., Kelleher, M., Kerkhof, A., Leenaars, A., Lönnqvist, J., Michel, K., Ostamo, A., Salander-Renberg, E., Sayil, I. Takahashi, Y., Van Heeringen, C., Värnik, A., & Wasserman, D. (1999). Suicide rates in the world: Update. *Archives of Suicide Research, 5, 1,* 81–89.

Schneider, C. D. (1992). *Shame, exposure, and privacy* (Rev. ed.). New York, NY/London, UK: W. W. Norton & Company, Inc.

Séguin, M., Lesage, A., & Kiely, M. C. (1995). Parental bereavement after suicide and accident: A comparative study. *Suicide and Life-Threatening Behavior, 25, 4,* 489–498.

Selakovic-Bursic, S. (2001). Reaching out to survivors of suicide: A column from Befrienders International. *Crisis: The Journal of Crisis Intervention and Suicide Prevention, 22, 1,* 47–48.

Shreve, B. W., & Kunkel, M. A. (1991). Self-psychology, shame, and adolescent suicide: Theoretical and practical considerations. *American Association Journal of Counseling & Development, 69, 4,* 305–311.

Silverman, E., Range, L., & Overholser, J. (1994–95). Bereavement from suicide as compared to other forms of bereavement. *Omega: Journal of Death and Dying, 30, 1,* 41–51.

Solomon, M. I. (1982–83). The bereaved and the stigma of suicide. *Omega: Journal of Death and Dying, 13, 4,* 377–387.

Stanard, R. P. (2000). Assessment and treatment of adolescent depression and suicidality. *Journal of Mental Health Counseling, 23, 3,* 204–217.

Stillion, J. M., & Stillion, B. D. (1998–99). Attitudes toward suicide: Past, present and future. *Omega: Journal of Death and Dying, 38, 3,* 77–97.

Stoelb, M., & Chiriboga, J. (1998). A process model for assessing adolescent risk for suicide. *Journal of Adolescence, 21, 4,* 359–370.

Tejedor, M. C., Díaz, A., Castillón, J. J., & Pericay, J. M. (1999). Attempted suicide: Repetition and survival – findings of a follow-up study. *Acta Psychiatrica Scandinavica, 100, 3,* 205–211.

Tekavcic-Grad, O., & Zavasnik, A. (1992). Aggression as a natural part of suicide bereavement. *Crisis: The Journal of Crisis Intervention and Suicide Prevention, 13, 2,* 65–69.

Thomas, S. P. (2003). From the editor–"Why did he do it?" Confronting issues of suicide and bereavement. *Issues in Mental Health Nursing, 24, 1,* 1–3.

Thompson, K. E., & Range, L. M. (1992). Bereavement following suicide and other deaths: Why support attempts fail. *Omega: Journal of Death and Dying, 26, 1,* 61–70.

Tisseron, S. (1992). *La honte: Psychanalyse d'un lien social.* Paris: Dunod.

Trolley, B. C. (1993). Kaleidoscope of aid for parents whose child died by suicidal and sudden, non-suicidal means. *Omega: Journal of Death and Dying, 27, 3,* 239–250.

Vajda, J., & Steinbeck, K. (2000). Factors associated with repeat suicide attempts among adolescents. *Australian and New Zealand Journal of Psychiatry, 34,* 437–445.

Valente, S. M., & Saunders, J. M. (1993). Adolescent grief after suicide. *Crisis: The Journal of Crisis Intervention and Suicide Prevention, 14, 1,* 16–22, 46.

Van Dongen, C. J. (1993). Social context of postsuicide bereavement. *Death Studies, 17, 2,* 125–141.

Van Ness, P. H., & Larson, D. B. (2002). Religion, senescence, and mental health: The end of life is not the end of hope. *The American Journal of Geriatric Psychiatry, 10, 4,* 386–397.

Vogels, W. (2003). *Becoming fully human: Living the Bible with God, each other and the environment* (Rev. ed.). Ottawa, ON: Novalis.

Wasserman, D. (1993). Alcohol and suicidal behavior. *Nordic Journal of Psychiatry, 47, 4,* 265–271.

Wertheimer, A. (1991). *A special scar: The experiences of people bereaved by suicide.* London, UK/New York, NY: Routledge.

Westefeld, J. S., Range, L. M., Rogers, J. R., Maples, M. R., Bromley, J. L., & Alcorn, J. (2000). Suicide: An overview. *The Counseling Psychologist, 28, 4,* 445–510.

Williams, J. M. G., & Pollock L. R. (1993). Factors mediating suicidal behaviour: Their utility in primary and secondary prevention. *Journal of Mental Health, 2, 1,* 3–26.

Woodward, K. L. (1970, April 6). How America lives with death. *Newsweek,* 81–88.

Yufit, R. I. (1991). American Association of Suicidology Presidential Address: Suicide assessment in the 1990's. *Suicide and Life-Threatening Behavior, 21, 2,* 152–163.

Zenit International News Agency [Z.I.N.A.]. (2003, Daily Dispatch/News Briefs, May 21). Adolescent suicides on the increase. (http://www.Zenit.org/english/ [Code: ZE03052106]).